Teaching History Today

TEACHING HISTORY TODAY AND IN THE FUTURE

About the Series

This series for K–12 and collegiate history teachers, educators, curriculum specialists, and preservice teacher education candidates provides information on current and future trends in the teaching and learning of history.

Books in the series explore the vast array of ideas, methods, and strategies that actively engage students in learning historical content and developing skills that will help them in their education and to become competent citizens.

The volumes are aimed at professionals working or planning to work in history education at all levels of education in schools and other venues related to the teaching of history.

About the Series Editor

The **Teaching History Today and in the Future** series was conceived by and is edited by Mark Newman, PhD, Professor of Social Studies Education, National College of Education, National Louis University, Chicago, Illinois.

Mark Newman has published articles and books on topics related to history, geography, and visual literacy. He received the 2022 Education Award from the International Visual Literacy Association and was awarded the National College of Education Distinguished Teaching Award in 2016. He has pursued his interest in history education through grants from the National Endowment for the Humanities and the Library of Congress Teaching with Primary Sources Program.

Titles in the Series

Teaching History Today: Applying the Triad of Inquiry, Primary Sources, and Literacy, by Mark Newman

New Approaches in Teaching History: Using Science Fiction to Introduce Students to New Vistas in Historical Thought, by Frederic Krome

Teaching History Today

Applying the Triad of Inquiry, Primary Sources, and Literacy

Mark Newman

ROWMAN & LITTLEFIELD
Lanham • Boulder • New York • London

Published by Rowman & Littlefield
An imprint of The Rowman & Littlefield Publishing Group, Inc.
4501 Forbes Boulevard, Suite 200, Lanham, Maryland 20706
www.rowman.com

86-90 Paul Street, London EC2A 4NE, United Kingdom

Copyright © 2024 by Mark Newman

All rights reserved. No part of this book may be reproduced in any form or by any electronic or mechanical means, including information storage and retrieval systems, without written permission from the publisher, except by a reviewer who may quote passages in a review.

British Library Cataloguing in Publication Information Available

Library of Congress Cataloging-in-Publication Data

Names: Newman, Mark, 1948– author.
Title: Teaching history today : applying the triad of inquiry, primary sources, and literacy / Mark Newman.
Description: Lanham : Rowman & Littlefield, [2024] | Series: Teaching history today and in the future | Includes bibliographical references. | Summary: "Teaching History Today is about placing inquiry, primary sources, and literacy foundations of history instruction front and center in the education. Readers can learn how to organize historical content into effective units, integrate the learning of content with development of skills, and gain expertise into engaging students collaboratively"—Provided by publisher.
Identifiers: LCCN 2023044591 (print) | LCCN 2023044592 (ebook) | ISBN 9781475868678 (cloth) | ISBN 9781475868685 (paperback) | ISBN 9781475868692 (epub)
Subjects: LCSH: History—Study and teaching—United States. | Inquiry-based learning—United States. | Culturally relevant pedagogy—United States.
Classification: LCC D16.3 .N44 2024 (print) | LCC D16.3 (ebook) | DDC 907.1—dc23/eng/2023120
LC record available at https://lccn.loc.gov/2023044591
LC ebook record available at https://lccn.loc.gov/2023044592

Contents

Acknowledgments	vii
Preface	ix
Introduction	1
Chapter 1: Inquiry-Based Learning	21
Chapter 2: Primary Sources	37
Chapter 3: Literacy	51
Chapter 4: Whose History?	69
Chapter 5: World History	87
Chapter 6: United States History	109
Chapter 7: The Local Community	135
Conclusion	149
About the Author	151

Acknowledgments

As every author knows, a book is a collaborative effort, the result of contributions from several people. In many ways, this book represents a synthesis of various efforts involving numerous people over many years. One person in particular deserves thanks. For many years, Gerry Danzer has been a mentor, colleague, and friend. This book is dedicated to him.

Another person deserving of thanks is Tom Koerner, my former editor at Rowman & Littlefield. He was a strong supporter of my work, offering sage advice and counsel. I would also like to thank Charles Harmon, Jasmine Holman, April Snider, and everyone else at Rowman & Littlefield for their help in making this book possible.

Lastly, I want to thank my wife Kim and my family for their love and support.

Preface

As this book neared completion, I observed a student teacher in an eighth-grade middle school U.S. history class. The lesson was toward the end of a unit on World War II. Student groups presented on the contributions of different groups to the war effort.

One group discussed the Austrian and German Jewish Americans in the Ritchie Boys project who interrogated Nazi prisoners of war and conducted counterintelligence. Another described the efforts of the Japanese American 442nd Infantry Regiment, the most decorated military unit in U.S. history. Next came the Navajo code talkers whose communications played a major role in many battlefield victories, including Iwo Jima. Students from one group were absent so the student teacher filled in, talking about the African American Tuskegee airmen who achieved unparalleled success in escorting bombers. At the end of the class, the student teacher asked if any of the students had prior knowledge of these groups. They all answered no.

The above lesson epitomizes effective history education in three ways. First, it applied an integrated triad of effective history teaching and learning: inquiry, primary source analysis, and literacy. Second, the lesson was culturally relevant. Third, the lesson met important state standards that are almost universally required nationally. Inquiry is mandated as the preferred method of teaching in 46 states. Cultural relevance is included in the standards of all 50 states.

Inquiry is the "how" of teaching and learning, collaboratively engaging students in studying history. As they inquire into a topic, students analyze primary sources, the "what" of historical content. Defined as the ability to read, think, and communicate, literacy is the skill set, another "how" of teaching and learning, that activates the inquiry process. Students apply these skills to read and analyze sources, manage information, and communicate findings.

Cultural relevance implies that learning has meaning for all students. Students learn best when they connect what is being learned to their lives and their backgrounds, so they see where they fit in history. Inquiry enhances relevance by including the narratives of different races, ethnicities, and genders in classroom instruction in a respectful way.

The purpose of this book is to explore how the inquiry, primary sources, and literacy triad promotes effective history teaching and learning in middle and high school history classes. A related purpose is to explore ways to use the triad to ensure what students learn is culturally relevant.

OVERVIEW OF THE BOOK

Teaching History Today: Applying the Triad of Inquiry, Primary Sources, and Literacy examines how this triad promotes effective, culturally relevant history education. It is written for middle and high school history preservice and classroom teachers and university history or social studies educators. The goals are to:

1. orient readers to the triad of inquiry, primary sources, and literacy as providing a viable strategy for effective, culturally relevant teaching and learning of history.
2. explore how and why the triad works in the 6–12 history classroom.
3. provide examples of classroom activities that apply the triad in culturally relevant and inclusive ways in the classroom.

Except for the introduction and conclusion, each chapter includes several suggested classroom activities.

Introduction

The book opens by discussing the current state of history education in middle and high school. Technology's impact on history is evaluated. The almost universal agreement regarding how history should be taught is contrasted with the growing history wars over what content students should learn. The importance of including diverse narratives is noted. The changing role and status of history in the 6–12 curriculum is examined, noting similarities and differences between middle and high school.

Chapter One: Inquiry-Based Learning

Inquiry opens the discussion of the triad by describing the inquiry process. The role of the Understanding by Design backward design model and the C3 Framework in the resurgence of inquiry is discussed. An alternative inquiry model developed by the author is also presented.

Chapter Two: Primary Sources

The world of primary sources is introduced, including defining what a primary source is. The incomplete, subjective nature of primary sources is discussed noting the promises and perils of classroom use. From print documents to the natural environment, the various types of primary sources are described.

Chapter Three: Literacy

Literacy is described as the skills set that makes inquiry and primary source analysis possible. The state of reading in Grades 6–12 in the United States is assessed. Also explored is the evolution over time from the concept of literacy to multiple literacies, including historical literacy. A method for developing a progressive reading process that climbs Bloom's revised taxonomy is presented as a way to improve student historical literacy skills over time.

Chapter Four: Whose History?

This chapter examines the organization of content to be more inclusive and culturally relevant for each student. The discussion revolves around a basic query of history: so what? That question focuses on significance and why we should care about history. An important aspect is increasing the relevance of what is being studied by ensuring students see themselves and their racial, ethnic, or gender groups in their studies. Another important method that increases relevance is using themes to connect the past to the present.

Chapter Five: World History

Chapter 5 examines what is likely the biggest challenge for teachers: organizing a course of study to help students learn about the history of the world. The history of world history in the schools is explored regarding how the world was defined for study over time. The current status of world history in the school curriculum is discussed. Various ways are presented to organize content so teaching and learning is more relevant and inclusive.

Chapter Six: United States History

Teaching about United States history follows a similar organization as chapter 5. It explores the history of the United States as a school subject over time, characterizing its status today. Various efforts over the last 80 years to revise the U.S. history curriculum are described. The chapter also discusses ways to ensure that teaching and learning is relevant to each student.

Chapter Seven: Local History

Integrating The Local Community suggests that a pivotal connection exists between the local community, the nation, and the world. The idea is to connect developments in the local community to U.S. and possibly world history. A major aspect is showing how studying the local community can help ensure students see themselves in their historical studies.

Conclusion

A brief synopsis of the book is presented.

Introduction

HISTORY EDUCATION IN PERSPECTIVE

In many states, history teachers face a difficult task. The nation's divisive political climate opened the current chapter of history culture wars between conservatives and liberals over what history content to teach. The general dispute concerns what version of U.S. history students should learn. Conservatives support a single master narrative of progress primarily by whites. Liberals back diverse, more inclusive narratives that explore positive and negative aspects of the nation's history. The current culture wars have dominated headlines and led to legal actions. Discussions over the content of history classes have affected almost every state.

A prime example is a debate that occurred in 2022 over the Florida Department of Education's (FDOE) professional development initiative connected to new state civics standards. While the Florida Commissioner of Education declares a "strong civic education is foundational to the American experience," the professional development focuses largely on history from a single perspective.[1]

According to a *Tampa Bay Times* article, most teachers agree with the new standards but have issues with how the state wants them to be taught. Teachers have criticized the state-sponsored professional development initiative for being skewed toward presenting Christian nationalist, conservative views exclusively. Ironically, the purported thrust behind this movement was to combat what Florida's governor saw as a leftist attempt to indoctrinate students. The FDOE issued a statement on the professional development initiative stating, "Every lesson we teach is based on history, not ideology or any form of indoctrination."[2]

Teachers dispute the FDOE claim on the absence of indoctrination. One teacher explained, "We are constantly under attack, and there is this false narrative that we're indoctrinating children, but that is nothing compared to what the state just threw in new civic educators' faces. That's straight-up indoctrination."[3] Another teacher who attended a state-sponsored conference in Jacksonville explained that presenters offered a single conservative interpretation of history as being the "correct way."[4] The teacher's concern was the lack of any other viewpoint being discussed.

The current history culture war is the noisiest voice in history education. It also can profoundly influence what content students learn. But other forces are also shaping history education for the present and the future, including technology and the subject of this book: the inquiry, primary sources, and literacy triad.

OVERVIEW

This introduction provides context for the chapters that follow by exploring the general state of history teaching and learning in Grades 6–12. The discussion opens by exploring two major influences on history education: the history culture wars and technology. Next, other national trends in history education are examined. State history standards provide insight into what teachers are required to teach. The U.S. history National Assessment of Educational Progress (NAEP), and the U.S. history advanced placement (AP) exam supply examples of content and methods. Thoughts on the future of history education close the discussion.

HISTORY WARS

Despite the tough rhetoric, the two sides in the culture wars have areas of agreement. Both sides generally agree that education should prepare students to become competent citizens. At least officially, both sides agree that history needs to be inclusive and culturally relevant for all students. Areas of disagreement include the purpose of history education, especially on what needs to be emphasized to educate effective citizens, meaning what content students should learn.

In a *New Yorker* article, historian David Blight posed questions that strike at the heart of the dispute:

> Should the discipline forge effective citizens? Should it be a source of patriotism? Should it thrive on analysis and argument, or be an art that emotionally moves us? Should it seek to understand a whole society, or be content to uncover that society's myriad parts?[5]

Blight answered yes to all the questions.

Neither side in the history wars adequately addresses all the needs identified by Blight. Each touts its own version of what history should be taught and learned. Conservatives support American exceptionalism, noting cultural pluralism exists but they favor a story of glorious progress by a distinctive and unique common, Anglo dominated culture. Liberals and progressives back a more diverse, inclusive, and less rosy picture that examines inequity and oppression but can also include advances and achievements.

An important consideration is that history wars are a global phenomenon. Argentina, Japan, Russia, and South Africa, among other nations, have had their own history culture wars. In each nation, a similar story plays out. The right backs a traditional viewpoint stressing the dominant culture. The left takes the opposite approach supporting diversity and a narrative often characterized by conflict.[6]

So whose story gets told? At this point, that question has no definitive answer but how the debate plays out can profoundly affect history education. Before explaining each of the two stances, historical context is needed because the current history culture war is just the latest chapter in a long-standing dispute.

The History of History Wars

History wars has been a continuing feature of history education since after the Civil War when a dispute arose over textbook coverage of the conflict. During World War I, the New York legislature banned textbooks containing what some considered seditious content or that glorified U.S. enemies in the war. In the 1920s, the issue was cultural pluralism versus the white supremacy of the Ku Klux Klan.[7] The 1930s and 1940s witnessed controversies over content relating to the support of communism.

After World War II, protests against the consensus school of history greatly expanded historical scholarship into racial, ethnic, and gender studies. In response, the content of history began to include social and economic themes and topics. Women and racial and ethnic groups slowly but surely were better integrated into the curriculum, textbooks, other materials, and classroom instruction.

In the early 1980s, another chapter of history wars began over exceptionalism, a common culture, and diversity. The first salvo was the 1983 publication of *A Nation at Risk*, which sounded an alarm about the quality of education in the United States. It recognized cultural pluralism but emphasized the idea of a common culture.

The 1990s witnessed several history war "battles." Controversies erupted over the 1994 National Standards for U.S. history and the 1998 California

History–Social Studies Framework.[8] Conservatives criticized the standards and the framework for being overly politically correct. In 1995, a dispute occurred over a proposed Smithsonian Institution Enola Gay exhibit. Should the exhibit focus solely on the American sacrifice in the war or include the devastating impact of the bomb in Japan, leading to neither.[9]

In the 21st century, reflecting the growing divisions in U.S. society, the debates over what to teach reemerged. As noted, those on the right support American exceptionalism. The most controversial idea on the left is critical race theory, though as we will see below, it does not really apply to history education in schools.

A Common Pattern

In the United States, Blight suggests that each history war follows a similar pattern. Politics and lack of knowledge play important roles. A dispute emerges carrying what Blight calls "visceral meaning for large swaths of the public."[10] School boards, state legislatures, and possibly the federal government debate aspects of history education. Hard lines are drawn as the strident rhetoric promises no surrender. Political sides organize. The media fuels the flames. Leaders in academia and other areas call for the latest research and findings. Over time the furor increases. Eventually, one side declares victory through a symbolic action such as removing a statue.

In the current struggle, the federal government and, more importantly, state legislatures take action to promote a certain point of view in the history curriculum. Eventually, a temporary respite from the wars occurs, resulting in good or bad history, depending upon your perspective. But there is no end. Often involving an aspect of the same issue, another history war emerges.

American Exceptionalism

The idea of American exceptionalism can be traced back to colonial times. Our purpose is to examine its current manifestation in the 21st century. The goal of the concept is to instill pride in Americans for the nation's achievements.

Ironically, the current phase of American exceptionalism arose in response to comments President Barack Obama made at a 2009 news conference in Europe. Responding to a question, Obama explained that he believed in American exceptionalism, adding that others probably had similar ideas about their own countries.

Obama provided a concise summary of what he meant by American exceptionalism that drew praise and sharp criticism from conservatives. Noting his pride in the United States, Obama explained, "We have a core set of values that are enshrined in our Constitution, in our body of law, in our democratic practices, in our belief in free speech and equality that, though imperfect, are exceptional." He also suggested that the United States plays an extraordinary role in the world but needs partners because the United States could not solve all the problems alone.[11]

Conservatives complained that while Obama identified important pillars of the exceptionalism credo, he contradicted the foundation of the concept as they defined it. Conservatives claim the founding of the nation based on natural rights gives the United States an ethos and culture that is unique among nations. Not only does the United States play a distinctive role in the world, but because of its purported superiority, the country can act in ways not acceptable for other nations.[12]

Critics of American exceptionalism argue that it is a myth that never did reflect reality. Geoffrey Hodgson suggested the idea of exceptionalism has been exaggerated. Hodgson claimed that the history of the United States has been much more connected to the rest of the world, especially Europe, then has often been assumed. Second, he noted that freedom and democracy have not developed smoothly and that gains have been fought for in the United States.[13]

A prominent topic of history wars debate today is race. Some supporters of American exceptionalism think examining the nation's history of racism is counterproductive.[14] Others on the left say that the exceptional quality of the United States has been the specter of racism.

Critical Race Theory

Critical race theory is the most recent concept in a long history of scholarship on race in the United States that can be traced back to colonial times. Over the last 120 years, numerous authors have commented on the primacy of race in the United States.[15] In the 1970s and 1980s, African American and other legal and political scholars of color developed critical race theory to explore race, racism, and the law in the post–civil rights era.

Critical race theory proponents state that the 1960s' civil rights legislation did not meet its goals, that racial injustice and racism continue to shape the nation's socioeconomic structure. They see institutions as perpetuating racism, pointing to laws, procedures, policies, regulations, and rules as the major forces maintaining white dominance. Derrick Bell, a founder of critical race theory, explained that "race is an indeterminate social construct that is continually reinvented and manipulated to maintain dominance and enhance white privilege."[16] Other authors emphasize that race is a social, not a biological, construct.[17]

Though critical race theory is widely recognized as a graduate level field of study, conservatives claim it is taught in K–12 schools. Teachers and other educators dispute that idea. Critical race theory itself is not taught in schools, but, in many schools, the trend is a toward a more diverse story of history that includes a critical look at the role race has played.

A primary influence has been the 1619 Project developed by Nikole Hannah-Jones for the *New York Times Magazine*. It offers "a new origin" story from the perspective of African Americans and slavery. For Hannah-Jones, 1619 is the birth date for the United States because the arrival of Africans set in motion what Jones called "its defining contradictions."[18] The 1619 Project has developed a podcast, audio book, a website with curricular materials, and a cable television series.

While garnering much praise, the 1619 Project has also elicited much criticism. Historians support the idea behind the project, noting the need for recognizing the central place of slavery and racism in U.S. history. But some historians on the left criticize Hannah-Jones for her interpretation of history. They dispute several of her claims, including that the nation was founded as a slaveocracy. Her contention that the movement for independence was fueled by rising antislavery attitudes in Great Britain also has been roundly attacked as has the idea that African Americans fought for their rights alone.[19]

Common sense indicates and ongoing historical scholarship has amply shown that indeed, Africans and African Americans fought against enslavement from its inception. In *African Founders*, David Hackett Fisher recounts numerous and continued ways that enslaved African Americans tirelessly initiated and spearheaded efforts to either gain their individual freedom or end slavery. Especially in the North, many of these efforts succeeded. But he also notes that they had help from whites who condemned slavery and its oppression.[20]

Conservatives also criticize the 1619 Project's interpretation of history. They attack it as being inaccurate and misguided. They reject the idea of the founders being dedicated to preserving slavery and that the founding date of the United States was 1619.[21]

The conservative reaction to the 1619 Project was part of an overall rejection of critical race theory. For our purposes, what is most important are the actions taken by state legislatures on the inclusion of critical race theory in school curricula. Since 2021, 44 states have introduced bills or taken actions to restrict teaching critical race theory or the discussion of racism in the classroom. As of March 2023, 18 states imposed bans and restrictions either through legislation or other avenues. Six have failed to pass laws against critical race theory.[22]

The Impact of History Wars

Several factors determine the parameters of teaching and learning history in schools. The current war over what history content is taught is one of those forces. In some states, the recent surge of legislation has tilted the balance scale toward some form of American exceptionalism celebrating ongoing progress. But widespread recognition exists of the role race has played in our history. For many, the question is how much exceptional progress should be the focus and what the context of the race discussion should be.

While history wars continue on a national stage, especially in the media, the extent of its influence is debatable. Other aspects of history education are playing as large or larger role in shaping teaching and history, including technology and a growing consensus on how the subject should be taught.

TECHNOLOGY

Technology's role in education generally, and in history specifically, mirrors its impact in society. Almost every facet of education has been affected in some way by technological advances. In many ways, technology has transformed teaching and learning, but, in other ways, it has been a bulwark of continuity.

As this book is being written, AI (artificial intelligence) apps, such as ChatGPT are raising concerns about who is doing student work. Students can type in a topic and the application spews out an essay. It is too early to evaluate the impact of such apps, but they do deserve mention.

Technology has revolutionized the ways we access and use information. It has the potential to transform teaching and learning when:

- technology is recognized as being another component in the teacher's toolkit instead of a panacea or miracle worker; and
- technology is integrated into a well-constructed, strategic plan of teaching and learning.

Like everything else in education, obstacles can reduce the viability of technology, including overuse, inadequate training in using tech, and a poor infrastructure that causes issues, among the things.

Benefits of Using Technology in the History Classroom

When used correctly and supported by an effective infrastructure, technology can significantly upgrade teaching and learning. Again, technology only works when it is part of an authentic educational experience that puts the student at the center of learning. It provides easy access to information and resources in multiple formats. Technology integrates what students do in everyday life into the classroom. It helps build a community of learners by promoting collaborative learning.

More specifically, technology improves teaching and learning in several ways. It promotes student interest and motivation to learn. In the classroom, students often use the same technology that they do outside school. Technology actively engages students, placing them at the center of the learning experience. It differentiates learning by allowing students to review resources until they gain greater understanding. Using diverse resources provides students with a more comprehensive view of what they study. And teachers can provide students with instant feedback.[23]

The presence of technology in the history classroom is increasing as is teacher proficiency in using it effectively. An important aspect is the rapidly growing number of easy-to-use apps that help teachers plan activities and assess student progress, often in real time. The apps also help students build important literacy and collaborative work skills.

Is technology the major driver of change in history education? The following discussion shows that technology is just one of several forces that are shaping the teaching and learning of history.

THE STATE OF HISTORY TEACHING AND LEARNING TODAY

As is true of education generally, history education has always been and is today a model for the historical theme of change and continuity. Knowledge of the content and of how people learn changes as do conditions, including political views. Similarly, changing times mean that students today are different in many ways from those in the past. An irony of the history culture wars is that the status of history and of social studies in the curriculum has declined, though that has been occurring for decades.

Amid all the changes, continuity also exists. In Grades 6–12, history remains the mainstay of the social studies curriculum but shares space with geography, civilization courses, civics and government, and possibly social sciences. The study of history is included in most of those courses.

Getting a national picture of the teaching and learning of history is difficult because some states either do not designate courses and grades or are vague in their descriptions. Generally states identify grade level subjects for Grades 6–8. For high school, the overwhelming majority of states provide descriptions of U.S. and world history courses but do not identify grade levels for teaching them. The sequencing of high school social studies courses is left to individual districts.

A survey of 30 states and the District of Columbia, where clear information was available, provides a broad overview of the 6–12 history curriculum. The survey shows that

- 30 states have a sequence of teaching world and U.S. history, with 12 states sequencing both subject areas across Grades 6–12; 12 states sequence only United States, and three do the same for world;
- in terms of years taught, 19 states offer more world than U.S. history, 6 provide equal time, and 5 teach U.S. history more than world; and
- 20 states have multiyear sequences. Sixteen states have two-year sequences in Grades 6–8 world (history, geography, and world civilizations), three offer a two-year course of study in Grades 6–8. In Grades 9–12, three states offer a two-year world and one has a two-year U.S. sequence.

The survey findings indicate that the majority of states have an orderly sequence of teaching and learning world and U.S. history across Grades 6–12. More time is spent on teaching the world than U.S. history in Grades 6–8. In high school, most states offer one-year courses for both world and United States history. But some important variations in the history curriculum exist that identify another area of continuity: the local character of history education.

History Education as a Local Affair

For good reasons, the local imperative makes for a disorderly national scene. But there is order in the disarray. We can visualize history education as an inverted pyramid. The national government and national professional associations exist at the top, spanning the nation. They provide policies, guidelines, and other services that filter down to the states, school districts, schools, and classrooms.

Numerous federal agencies have programs to support history education, including the U.S. Department of Education, the National Endowment for the Humanities, the National Archives, the Library of Congress, and the Teaching American History grants, among others. Professional associations and other entities have also had a national impact. The National Council for the Social Studies C3 Framework influences state standards, helping inquiry become the preferred method of teaching and learning. The Common Core Literacy Standards also are influential. Gilder Lehrman and other entities also provide resources and professional development.

States occupy the next level and oversee all levels of public education. The governor, the state legislature, and the state office or department of education are responsible for the state's educational enterprise. An important state task is the development of standards that describe what students are to learn at different grades and often how they go about that learning. Many states reference the C3 Framework or Common Core as an influence and list the Library of Congress as a teacher resource.

Historically and today, the diverse conditions in states, local communities, and even within school districts make education generally and history education specifically a local affair. For example, in the eastern United States, colonization centers around the British and French, perhaps the Dutch in New York. In Louisiana, French colonization is a major focus while in California and the Southwest, Spanish efforts are important. In some states, indigenous history is an important part of the curriculum.

Demographics and politics also play a role in developing the history curriculum for a state. The growing emphasis on student-centered learning includes making sure what students learn is relevant to them. Relevance implies connecting what is learned to the student's everyday life and also ensuring that racial, ethnic, and gender groups are equitably studied.

The upshot is that students may study similar or different topics nationwide, in a state, or even in a district. They also may conduct the study from varying perspectives. Race, ethnicity, possibly religion, gender, and local context influence what students study. Basically, where you live and where you teach influences what history is taught and possibly how it is learned. These decisions are guided by state history/social studies standards.

State Standards and History Education

History is often included as part of the social studies standards. A review of all 50 states and the District of Columbia showed that state standards can serve as the social studies curriculum, with history embedded within the larger social studies standards construct. Typically, state education offices form a committee of teachers and other educators to craft draft standards. The drafts are disseminated for review, revised, and then published in final form.

While some similarities exist among the state standards, differences also abound. Though history education is centered around the United States and world, many states have a strong state history component. Another distinction concerns the details or lack thereof in the standards. Some standards are detailed, specifying grade-level subjects and identifying important content topics to be taught. Or the standards are vague and confusing, providing little insight into courses or content, leaving those decisions to local school districts.

Some states have been purposely vague in their standards for a couple of reasons. On one hand, local districts need flexibility. On the other hand, if the standards are too detailed, the concern is that teachers will only teach the content listed in the standard. The Kentucky social studies standards explicitly state that the standards are not the curriculum. Instead, they show what students should master by the end of the grade or grade span. As for how those goals are met, the decisions are left to the schools and teachers.

Regarding the content of the U.S. history standards, a 2021 study of state standards by the Fordham Institute commented,

> The U.S. history standards focus on what happened and why and do not sacrifice historical context to present-day relevance, ahistorical moral judgment, or an excessive emphasis on students' personal perspective. The standards communicate that interpretations depend on supporting evidence in historical context and that all interpretations are therefore not equally valid.[24]

The state standards follow recent scholarship and ideas in history education. Most important for our purposes are requirements for inquiry, primary sources, and literacy.

Inquiry

In almost every state, inquiry is the preferred or required teaching and learning method. The Tennessee history standards state the following:

> Teachers should center instruction on inquiry-based models, which require students to engage in critical thinking, self-assessment, reasoning, problem-solving, collaboration, and investigation in order to make connections in new and innovative ways as they progress through social studies education.[25]

Other states mandate inquiry in various ways. Some divide their social studies standards into two categories. Illinois organizes standards into inquiry skills and disciplinary concepts. Others integrate inquiry into the standards. Michigan has a standard on historical inquiry and analysis.[26]

Primary Sources

The use of primary sources is also encouraged with many states noting them in their standards. In Colorado, history standards for sixth grade require students to analyze and interpret primary and secondary sources. In Alabama, the use of primary sources is stressed.[27]

The introduction to the 2018 Massachusetts History and Social Studies Framework has two appendices for using primary sources. The framework connects inquiry to primary sources. One purpose of the high school United States history standards is to "strengthen their ability to develop research questions and conduct inquiries by interpreting primary sources."[28]

Literacy

Virtually every state standards document with any detail underscores the central role literacy plays in history teaching and learning. Literacy is integrated into the standards in various ways. As shown above in the primary sources discussion, literacy terms such as *analyze* and *interpret* are part of the standards. Wyoming and Washington reference the Common Core literacy standards for social studies, Grades 6–12. Arkansas, California, and Indiana have separate literacy standards.[29]

What the State Standards Tell Us about the Teaching and Learning of History

As is often true in history, while the state standards tell us much about history education, they also raise many questions. And there are some important caveats that need noting. The local character of education means statements on the teaching and learning of history do not apply universally. The state standards give an incomplete view of history education, especially at the classroom level. In some states, the standards are being revised so the documents available for our discussion may not fully apply in the near future. And there is the question of how closely teachers and schools pay attention to the standards.

What do the standards tell us? First, while they do not form a national history curriculum for Grades 6–12, the standards have enough in common to provide some general foundational elements. Agreement exists across the nation regarding what subjects to teach and what is the preferred instructional method. World, United States, and possibly state history comprise the core of the 6–12 history curriculum. Inquiry is the preferred, often required, method of teaching and learning generally involving primary source analysis and development of literacy skills.

Equally important, some the standards cited above work against the idea of teaching single perspective to students. In Michigan, the conclusion to the United States history and geography standards states that "historical and geographic literacy demands that students learn to read critically; analyze and evaluate arguments; and decide which positions, given the evidence, are more or less plausible, better or worse."[30]

Second, while history education may be considered a state and local school district affair, it is strongly influenced by national organizations and agencies.

References to inquiry as the preferred method of instruction often cite the NCSS *C3 Framework*. In discussing suggested resources for primary sources, many states note the Library of Congress, among others. And literacy skills development is often based on the Common Core Standards.

Third, state standards change over time, so some are more up to date than others. States either mandate standards review or revision according to a timetable or the changes happen as needed. In the survey referenced above, some standards were over 10 years old while others were new. Where standards have been in place for at least 8–10 years, it is possible that school districts have already updated their history curricula to accommodate new ideas, trends, and needs.

NAEP AND ADVANCED PLACEMENT

Two prominent national assessments are the National Assessment of Educational Progress (NAEP) and advanced placement (AP) exams. Neither provide a comprehensive or accurate assessment of all history students in Grades 6–12, nor do they claim to do so. They do supply snapshots of important components of history teaching and learning.

NAEP

NAEP only assesses U.S. history in eighth grade. The 2018 exam was administered to 16,400 students from 780 schools nationwide; 15,100 were enrolled in public schools and 1,200 in private schools. That year, 3,893,000 students were enrolled in eighth grade.[31] The NAEP exam tries to reflect classroom practices. The NAEP U.S. history framework provides important information on history teaching and learning today. How well does the description below compare to what you have seen in schools?

NAEP organizes its assessment around themes, chronological periods, and cognitive skills. There are four themes. Democracy in the United States stresses change and continuity in ideas, institutions, key figures, controversies, and events. Culture is defined as the meeting and interactions of peoples, cultures, and ideas. Technology focuses on technological and economic changes and their connection to society, the environment, and ideas. The world role explores the changing role of the United States in the world.

The eight, at times overlapping, chronological periods are as follows:

1. Beginnings to 1607.
2. Colonization, settlement, and communities (1607 to 1763).
3. The Revolution and the new nation (1763 to 1815).

4. Expansion and reform (1801 to 1861).
5. Crisis of the Union: Civil War and Reconstruction (1850 to 1877).
6. The development of modern America (1865 to 1920).
7. Modern America and the World Wars (1914 to 1945).
8. Contemporary America (1945 to present).[32]

The last component is the "cognitive dimension of the assessment."[33] There are two ways of thinking and knowing about U.S. history: historical knowledge and perspective and historical analysis and interpretation. They are skills-based and represent a progression of cognitive skills: basic, proficient, and advanced. The cognitive domains emphasize actively engaging students in learning.

Historical knowledge and perspectives assess the students' general conceptual understanding of U.S. history. Among other things, it includes "knowing about and understanding people, concepts, themes, historical sources, sequencing events, identifying multiple perspectives, and considering history through the eyes of different groups."[34]

Historical analysis and interpretation moves to higher cognitive levels. It ranges from explaining issues and recognizing historical patterns to establishing cause-and-effect relationships and establishing significance. Also involved are assessing evidence to draw conclusions and communicating insightful accounts of the past.[35]

The U.S. history exam has two types of questions. Selected response requires participants to read a question and choose the most correct option. The format includes matching, grid, zone, multiple response, and in-line choices. Constructed response requires a written or oral response to a question. Generally, questions provide students with a visual (picture, map, table, etc.) or a list of options relevant to answering the questions. The questions assume that students possess the literacy skills and content knowledge to answer correctly. Reflecting skills categories, questions ranged from basic to proficient to advanced.

A sample basic multiple choice question asked student to identify a secondary source from a list of four choices. The options included the following:

- a Russian woman's account of escaping from Russia in 1992
- a 1924 anti-immigration newspaper editorial
- the story of a Greek family coming to the United States in 1906 written by a journalist in 1955
- U.S. census data on immigration

Almost one-third answered the question correctly, choosing the journalist's story of the Greek immigrant family.

A higher-level multiple choice question presented students with a Civil War recruitment poster for African Americans (called people of color in the poster). They were asked in what war was the poster asking them to fight. Students used evidence in the poster to make inferences about the war. Sixty-three percent of students answered the question correctly.

A constructed response question asked students to evaluate the following statement: "The South could never have won the Civil War."[36] Students were presented with a table on resources possessed by the North and the South including population, railroads, farm acreage, and factory workers. Ten percent of eighth graders answered the question appropriately, meaning they identified two or more reasons in their answers. Most students (63%) had a partial answer.

What does NAEP tell us about history teaching and learning today? Teaching and learning is organized around themes and a chronology that integrates the learning of content with the building of historical thinking and literacy skills that climb Bloom's revised taxonomy. Students are actively engaged in their learning using a variety of primary and secondary source documents. They also learn to distinguish between these two types of documents. NAEP is now an online assessment, reflecting another trend in history education.

Examining the NAEP U.S. history assessment supplies pieces to the puzzle that is history education today. The Advanced Placement (AP) tests in history contribute a few more pieces.

Advanced Placement

The advanced placement (AP) history programs also provide a snapshot of relevant aspects of history teaching and learning. For comparison purposes, we look at the U.S. history advanced placement course and test.

In 2022, 460,000 students worldwide took the AP U.S. History (APUSH) exam. AP U.S. history is a one-year introductory college-level course with a capstone exam that can provide students with college credit. Students explore various historical concepts by analyzing historical sources, making connections, and developing historical arguments.[37] The content is organized by chronological historical periods (units), themes, and historical thinking skills.

There are nine units of varying lengths ranging from 8 to 21 class periods. They are identified by the time period studied. Each unit is divided into subtopics. Prominent themes include "American and national identity; work, exchange, and technology; geography and the environment; migration and settlement; politics and power; America in the world; American and regional culture; and social structures." Units stress one or more of these themes.

Period 7: 1890–1945 emphasizes two themes: (1) politics and power and (2) geography and the environment.[38]

Reflecting the AP test questions, unit assessments include multiple choice, short answer, and free responses that are either document-based questions (DBQ) or long essays. The AP use of the DBQ influenced this assessment's integration into 6–12 history education. DBQs are inquiry-based, involve analysis of document excerpts and visuals, and develop literacy skills.

The AP U.S. history discussion provides more pieces to the teaching and learning of history puzzle, confirming findings from examining state standards and NAEP. History education in Grades 6–12 actively engages students in their studies. The triad of inquiry-based learning, primary sources, and literacy integrates content learning with progressive skills development.

CONCLUSION

So what future trends are evident? As this book is being written, there are some salient characteristics of history education. First, technology will play an increasingly important role in historical scholarship and the teaching and learning of history. Second, agreement exists on several important matters. The goal of history education remains educating competent citizens. Teaching and learning needs to be culturally relevant so it is meaningful for all students. Students need to be actively engaged in their learning. The triad of inquiry-based learning, primary sources, and literacy is the preferred, indeed the required instructional method.

The unknown factors are the eventual outcome of the history culture wars and the impact of technology, especially AI applications. The crux of the history wars debate concerns what content students study and what the ultimate purpose is. Are students to learn about American exceptionalism, celebrating progress without critically questioning the past and possibly the present? Or are students to study diverse stories that include the positive and negative aspects of history by critically examining the past and the present? Regarding technology, use is likely to expand and be enhanced by new innovations. How far these innovations go remains to be seen.

One indicator of the future is that the idea of teaching a single perspective contradicts the strong thrust for critical thinking and decision making in state standards. The purpose here is to explore the current and possibly future role inquiry-based learning, primary sources, and literacy play in history education for Grades 6–12.

NOTES

1. "Governor Ron DeSantis Announces Florida Students' Elevating Their Excellence in Civics," news release, June 30, 2022, https://flgov.com/2022/06/30/governor-ron-desantis-announces-florida-students-elevating-their-excellence-in-civics/.
2. Ana Ceballos and Sommer Brugal, "Some Teachers Alarmed by Florida Civics Training Approach on Religion, Slavery," *Tampa Bay Times*, July 1, 2022, https://www.tampabay.com/news/florida-politics/2022/06/28/some-teachers-alarmed-by-florida-civics-training-approach-on-religion-slavery/.
3. Ceballos and Brugal, "Some teachers alarmed."
4. Travis Gibson, "Florida Teachers Raise Concerns about New Civics Training, Say It Downplays Slavery, Promotes Originalism," News4JAX, June 30, 2022, https://www.news4jax.com/news/local/2022/06/29/florida-teachers-raise-concerns-about-new-civics-training-say-it-downplays-slavery-promotes-originalism/.
5. David. W. Blight, "The Fog of History Wars," *The New Yorker*, June 9, 2021, n.p., https://www.newyorker.com/news/daily-comment/the-fog-of-history-wars.
6. Tony Taylor and Robert Guyver (eds.)., *History Wars and the Classroom: Global Perspectives* (Charlotte, NC: Information Age Publishing, Inc., 2012), 12.
7. Jonathan Zimmerman, "Each 'Race' Could Have Its Heroes Sung": Ethnicity and the History Wars in the 1920s," *The Journal of American History* 87, no. 1 (June 2000): 92–111.
8. On the debate over the California standards, see Gary B. Nash and Ross Dunn, *History on Trial: Culture Wars and the Teaching of the Past* (New York: Knopf, 1997); and James Andrew LaSpina, *California in a Time of Excellence: School Reform at the Crossroads of the American Dream* (New York: SUNY Press, 2009), 12.
9. Richard H. Kohn, "History and the Culture Wars: The Case of the Smithsonian Institution's Enola Gay Exhibition," *The Journal of American History* 82, no. 3 (December 1995): 1036–1063.
10. Blight, "The Fog of History Wars."
11. "News Conference by President Obama, 4/04/2009," The White House, Office of the Press Secretary, https://obamawhitehouse.archives.gov/the-press-office/news-conference-president-obama-4042009.
12. Mike Gonzalez and Jonathan Burch, "Restore the Teaching of American Exceptionalism in the Classroom," August 28, 2020, https://www.heritage.org/education/commentary/restore-the-teaching-american-exceptionalism-the-classroom, Kim R. Holmes, "Why American Exceptionalism Is Different from Other Countries' 'Nationalisms,'" The Heritage Foundation, September 29, 2020, https://www.heritage.org/american-founders/lecture/why-american-exceptionalism-different-other-nations-nationalisms.
13. See the preface for Geoffrey Hodgson, *The Myth of American Exceptionalism* (New Haven: Yale University Press, 2010).
14. Scott Warren, "The Myth of American Exceptionalism," *The Baltimore Sun*, March 12, 2021, https://www.baltimoresun.com/opinion/op-ed/bs-ed-op-0314-american-exceptionalism-myth-20210312-2gs22qtfvjhrfaercjhvv4hbby-story.html.

15. Numerous authors have explored race in U.S. history. Some examples over time include W. E. B. DuBois, *The Souls of Black Folk* (New York: Bantam Books 1989, originally published 1903); Carter Woodson, "The Mis-Education of the Negro" (Lawrenceville, NJ: Africa World Press, 2006, originally published 1933); Gunnar Myrdal, *An American Dilemma: The Negro Problem and Modern Democracy*, volume 1 (New York: Routledge, 1995, originally published 1944); Winthrop Jordan, *White Over Black: American Attitudes toward the Negro, 1550–1812* (London: Oxford University Press, 1968); and Isabel Wilkerson, *Caste: The Origins of Our Discontents* (New York: Penguin Random House, 2020).

16. Derrick Bell, *Race, Racism, and American Law*, fourth edition (Gaithersburg, NY: Aspen Publishers, 2000), 16.

17. David Kaplan, *Navigating Ethnicity: Segregation, Placemaking, and Difference* (Lanham, MD: Rowman & Littlefield, 2018), 11.

18. Hannah-Jones Nikola, "The 1619 Project," *The New York Times Magazine* (August 18, 2019), 4.

19. Adam Serwer, "The Fight over the 1619 Project Is Not about the Fact," *The Atlantic*, December 23, 2019, https://www.theatlantic.com/ideas/archive/2019/12/historians-clash-1619-project/604093/.

20. David Hackett Fisher, *African Founders: How Enslaved People Expanded American Ideals* (New York: Simon & Schuster, 2022).

21. L. Morel, "A Review of the 1619 Project Curriculum," December 15, 2020, https://www.heritage.org/progressivism/report/review-the-1619-project-curriculum; Mitch McConnell, "READ: McConnell Letter to the Education Department Regarding '1619 Project' Programs," CNN, April 30, 2021, https://www.cnn.com/2021/04/30/politics/mitch-mcconnell-miguel-cardona-letter/index.html.

22. Sarah Schwartz, "Map: Where Critical Race Theory Is under Attack," Education Week, June 11, 2021, updated March 21, 2023, https://www.edweek.org/policy-politics/map-where-critical-race-theory-is-under-attack/2021/06.

23. Mrs. Oyewale, Gbemisola Mary, and Jonathan Oluropo Familugba, "The Use of Technology in Teaching and Learning History in Secondary Schools," *American Journal of Multidisciplinary Research & Development* 3, no. 6 (June 2021): 43–48.

24. Jeremy A. Stern, Alison E. Brody, Jose A. Gregory, Stephen Griffith, and Jonathan Pulvers, *State of State Standards for Civics and U.S. History in 2021* (Washington DC: Thomas B. Fordham Institute. June 2021), 364; https://fordhaminstitute.org/national/research/state-state-standards-civics-and-us-history-2021.

25. Tennessee Department of Education, *Social Studies Standards* (2017), p. 2; https://www.tn.gov/content/dam/tn/education/standards/ss/Social_Studies_Standards.pdf.

26. Illinois State Board of Education, *Illinois Social Studies Standards* (Springfield: Illinois State Board of Education, 2017); Michigan Department of Education, *Draft Michigan K–12 Standards Social Studies* (Ann Arbor: Michigan Department of Education, 2018), https://www.michigan.gov/-/media/Project/Websites/mde/2018/06/21/SS_May_2018_Public_Final.pdf?rev=cdbb65f2106e4b9888a723d430e35522.

27. Colorado Department of Education, *Social Studies* (2023), https://www.cde.state.co.us/cosocialstudies; Curriculum and Instruction Section, Alabama Department

of Education, *Alabama Course of Study: Social Studies* (Montgomery, AL: Alabama Department of Education, 2010), 7.

28. Massachusetts Department Elementary and Secondary Education, *History and Social Science Framework: Grades Pre-Kindergarten to 12* (Springfield: Massachusetts Department Elementary and Secondary Education. 2018), 117.

29. Wyoming Department of Education, Social Studies (Cheyenne: Wyoming Department of Education, 2018), https://edu.wyoming.gov/for-district-leadership/standards/social-studies/; Washington Office of Superintendent and Public Instruction, Social Studies Learning Standards, 2018, https://www.k12.wa.us/sites/default/files/public/socialstudies/standards/OSPI_SocStudies_Standards_2019.pdf; Division of Elementary and Secondary Education, *Social Studies Standards and Courses* (Little Rock, AR: Division of Elementary and Secondary Education, 2022), https://dese.ade.arkansas.gov/Offices/learning-services/curriculum-support/social-studies-standards-and-courses; California State Board of Education, *California Common Core State Standards English Language Arts and Literacy in History/Social Studies, Science, and Technical Subjects* (Sacramento: California State Board of Education, 2013); Indiana Department Education, *Social Studies* (Bloomington: Indiana Department Education, 2020), https://www.in.gov/doe/students/indiana-academic-standards/social-studies/.

30. Michigan Department of Education, *Draft Michigan –K-12 Standards Social Studies*, p. 63.

31. National Center for Education Statistics, U.S. Department of Education and the Institute of Education Sciences, *NAEP Report Card: U.S. History. The Nation's Report Card* (2018), https://www.nationsreportcard.gov/ushistory/about/assessment-framework-design/.

32. National Center for Education Statistics, *NAEP Report Card.*

33. National Center for Education Statistics, *NAEP Report Card.*

34. National Center for Education Statistics, *NAEP Report Card.*

35. National Center for Education Statistics, *NAEP Report Card.*

36. National Center for Education Statistics, *NAEP Report Card.*

37. The College Board, *AP United States History: The Course* (New York: The College Board, 2022), https://apcentral.collegeboard.org/courses/ap-united-states-history/course.

38. The College Board, *AP United States History: The Course.*

Chapter 1

Inquiry-Based Learning

In recent years, many history teachers faced a similar dilemma. They realized that their go-to methods, often direct instruction or the obligatory DBQ (document-based question), were not working well. Students were not motivated to learn because they thought the activities were boring. Most importantly, student performance was underwhelming. A common theme is that switching to inquiry-based learning (IBL) greatly improved their teaching and student learning. Some teachers recounted their experiences in journal articles.[1] But others have commented on blogs and other online posts.

Two blog posts in particular offer insight into why teachers switched to inquiry-based learning. Alison, a New York history teacher with 17 years of classroom experience—first in middle school and later in high school advanced placement U.S. history—explained that she used to write simple DBQs. On her blog, *Peacefield History*, named after John Adams's house, she commented that the DBQs were boring for her and for the students. With the basic DBQs, "students were simply showing that they comprehended the historical documents and that they could summarize. While those are important skills, they challenge students at a very basic level."[2]

Switching to inquiry transformed her teaching and student learning. She commented that because inquiry-based learning "mimics" authentic historical inquiry, students were thinking about history. They considered how history occurred, who was responsible for change, and how what happened should be remembered. Conducting inquiry improved her students' content knowledge. Equally important, inquiry differentiated learning, especially for students with special needs.[3]

Another blogger, Erin, a national board-certified high school social studies teacher in Washington state, discussed creating inquiry-based learning in social studies. She summarized prior methods of teaching and learning, suggesting many high school history classes revolved around memorization, movies, or both. What was not involved were what she called "wondering, investigation, grey area, or multiple right answers" that currently are the "core of teaching these courses well."[4] The implication was that inquiry-based learning included those core areas and led to better student performance.

This chapter explores the inquiry-based learning (IBL) component of the triad, seeking answers to three questions:

1. How do we define inquiry-based learning?
2. How is inquiry-based learning being used today in teaching and learning history in Grades 6–12?
3. How has technology impacted the use of inquiry-based learning in history in Grades 6–12, including thoughts on the future role of technology?

AGED WINE IN NEW BOTTLES

In many ways, the current vogue in inquiry-based learning represents the most recent vintage of a practice that dates back over 150 years. Edward Austin Sheldon was a follower of the Swiss educator-reformer Johann Pestalozzi. He founded the Oswego (New York) school of teaching in the mid-1800s. In an annual report to the Oswego Board of Education in 1860, Sheldon explained his philosophy of education:

> In this plan of studies the object is not so much to impart information as to educate the senses, and awaken a spirit of inquiry. To this end the pupils must be encouraged to do most of the talking and acting. They must be allowed to draw their own conclusions, and if wrong, led to correct them.[5]

During the 20th century, inquiry went in and out of vogue. It often competed unsuccessfully with lecture as the preferred method of teaching and learning history, though strong advocates remained committed to inquiry. Fast forward to the late 20th and early 21st centuries. Advances in the knowledge of the brain, changing ideas on how students best learn, alterations in the demographics of the student population, and accountability led to more student-centered teaching and learning.

A culmination occurred in 2013 when the National Council for the Social Studies C3 Framework acknowledged rising trends in social studies education. The C3 Framework centers social studies teaching and learning around an inquiry arc.[6] Today, inquiry is the required or preferred teaching and learning method in social studies/history standards of almost every state.

Technology has been a major factor in the emergence of inquiry. Without the internet, the C3 Framework would have had a harder time achieving almost universal acceptance of inquiry as the preferred method of teaching and learning history. The digitization of documents and online sites provide teachers with easy access to resources and professional development venues offered by such sites as the Library of Congress. Virtually everything educational, including blog posts, can be accessed with a simple search and click of a mouse button. Technology also makes it possible to survey states to examine where inquiry fits in the Grades 6–12 history curriculum.

THE STATUS OF INQUIRY IN THE GRADES 6–12 HISTORY CURRICULUM

A survey of the departments of education of the 50 states and the District of Columbia found that 46 states explicitly mandate inquiry. As a result, no matter what side a state may take in the history culture wars, they embrace inquiry-based learning as the preferred method of teaching and learning history. For example, the 2023 version of the Florida social studies standards prominently feature inquiry.[7]

A major goal of inquiry-based learning is to educate students to become independent learners who assume responsibility for their education and their civic lives. The remainder of this chapter explores how inquiry-based learning helps teachers achieve that goal.

INQUIRY-BASED LEARNING

Basically, inquiry is investigation. It is used in various disciplines but as Levy et al. observed, it has subject matter specific parameters. In science, inquiry investigates and collects data related to explaining natural world phenomena. In history education, inquiry provides students with opportunities to conduct their own investigations into past events and people.[8]

Inquiry-based learning provides the framework for student investigations. It is the structure of teaching and learning history, a methodological construct that helps clean up the messiness of history by providing focus and direction for student learning.

This section explores inquiry-based learning by answering three questions:

1. What is inquiry-based learning?
2. How does inquiry-based learning work? This query also delves into its strengths and weaknesses.
3. How can inquiry-based learning be implemented in the 6–12 history classroom?

WHAT IS INQUIRY-BASED LEARNING?

Inquiry-based learning is much more than just posing and answering questions. Its results extend beyond gaining understanding. IBL is a strategically plotted program of learning that actively engages students in historical investigations to improve their content knowledge and build skills over time. It also helps students understand the relevance of what they are learning and to connect what they study to their lives. In the process, students gain content understanding and skills competency they will use throughout their lives. Often IBL builds social-emotional skills as students work together to explore topics and come to conclusions.

At its core, IBL is a skills-based approach. The skills are connected to various components of the inquiry process applied at the course, unit, lesson, or activity level. As students practice the inquiry process over time, they become more knowledgeable, more competent, and more independent.

Several studies have identified the cognitive processes involved in historical inquiry. Some stress studying a primary source document but often extend beyond that task. Voet and DeWever summarized the findings of several studies, identifying five cognitive processes involved in historical inquiry: sourcing, appraising, specifying, constructing, and arguing. In turn, a variety of skills are connected to these processes, including summarizing, comparing, corroborating, contextualizing, and evaluating.[9]

Based on the findings of Voet and DeWever, Table 1.1 provides an overview of the five cognitive processes. While not comprehensive, the table shows the range of skills that students develop by engaging in inquiry. Note that the cognitive processes presented in the table move from exploring a document to developing conclusions based on conducting inquiry.

Because IBL stresses skills, teachers can develop a progressive learning sequence to measure student performance and improvement over time. The sequence can be differentiated and applied at different levels depending upon student competency. Based on practice at progressive levels of proficiency, students climb Bloom's revised taxonomy. The ultimate goal is to have students independently conduct a historical inquiry investigation.

To sum up, inquiry-based learning is a strategically crafted teaching and learning program focused on skills development over time that improves content understanding. The same skills are applied consistently throughout the course as students learn different content. Inquiry also helps teachers organize content into manageable amounts for students to study a topic in some depth. Whether it be a course or unit, the very process of organization means teachers decide what students will or will not learn. We gain insight into how inquiry impacts what students learn by looking at how it works.

Table 1.1. Cognitive Processes Involved in Historical Inquiry

Sourcing	Establishing the provenance (author, title, place, date of creation, publisher)
	Determining type and nature of historical source
	Evaluating a source's reliability, trustworthiness, and connection to the topic
Appraising	Analyzing intentions and purposes of the author in creating the source
	Identifying biases, beliefs
	Identifying message of source, comparing to other sources
	Evaluating accuracy and evidence supporting claims
Specifying	Asking questions to guide understanding
	Drawing on prior knowledge
	Evaluating incompleteness and seeking more information
Constructing	Establishing place and time context, creating chronology of events
	Making inferences related to topic and questions
	Developing explanations to answer questions
Arguing	Developing an argument based on evidence

HOW DOES INQUIRY-BASED EARNING WORK?

For inquiry-based learning to work effectively, the classroom must become a collaborative community of learners with the teacher and the students contributing to the learning process. Students work together on various activities to reach a common objective. Classroom rules, policies, and procedures regulate behavior so students feel safe and secure to voice their opinions. Building community facilitates students learning to engage in inquiry.

Models of Inquiry-Based Learning

Various models of inquiry-based learning exist. Some have been developed by teachers and educators to meet specific classroom needs. National organizations also have developed more general models. Two models have been most influential. Jay McTighe and Grant Wiggins developed the Understanding by Design™ (UbD) backward design model that applies to all subject areas.[10] The National Council for the Social Studies Inquiry Arc is the core of its C3 Framework. The Inquiry Arc was later supplemented by the Inquiry Design Model.[11]

Both UbD and the Inquiry Arc/Inquiry Design Model have received much attention. They will be briefly discussed here as will an IBL model developed by the author. But first a short note on terminology regarding questions and the centrality of questioning in inquiry-based learning. McTighe and Wiggins use the term essential question and the C3 Framework uses compelling question for the same thing: the overarching query that frames the investigation.

Why there are two names for the same type of question is a mystery to this author. Please remember these terms are interchangeable. Because the focus is on history, we use the wording of the C3 Framework, namely the compelling question.

The Central Role of the Compelling Question

Another similarity of all inquiry models is that questioning is at the heart of learning. Compelling questions in particular have garnered much attention. An excellent compelling question can lead to an exciting and rewarding learning experience. A poorly phrased compelling question can have the opposite effect.

A compelling question should have certain qualities, including the following:

- focusing on the highest-level cognitive skills appropriate for the students
- encompassing all of the content of the unit
- simple phrasing
- the question requires more than a yes or a no answer.

McTighe and Wiggins describe essential (compelling) questions as engaging students in making meaning so they can develop a deeper understanding of important concepts. They stress that an essential question cannot be answered in a single class period.[12] Referring to an excellent compelling question, S. G. Grant describes it as being "intellectually meaty" so that it addresses an enduring issue, debate, or concern in social studies. He suggests "Was the American Revolution revolutionary?" works as a compelling question. It indicates that the discussion continues on the nature of the revolution, and it can be studied across the entire unit.[13]

Grant's phrasing raises some concerns. This author's take on the phrasing of a compelling question is somewhat different. A compelling question cannot be answered with a yes or no response, but students could answer Grant's example with a yes or no. It needs a higher-level interrogative such as *why* or perhaps *how* and *why* to activate higher-level thinking skills.

Grant also states that the compelling question must be student friendly, hitting at the core of the effective question.[14] The question must have relevance to the student. For example, exploring whether the American Revolution was revolutionary will lead students to investigate ideas and concerns relevant to them such as rights. In addition, the question must not be above the ability of the student to answer it. The question should be simple and straightforward using vocabulary appropriate for the students.

The compelling question should have the following components:

1. A high-level interrogative such as why or how and why that identifies the task.
2. A clearly stated topic.
3. Possibly examples that are subtopics, themes, or other aspects that will be used to answer the compelling question. In some cases, the topic is also the example.

For example, in a high school U.S. history course, a compelling question on the American Revolution might be this: "Regarding its effects on the United States politically, economically, and socially, how revolutionary was the American Revolution?" It adapts Grant's question by providing more details. The how identifies the task while the topic is whether the effects of the American Revolution on the United States were revolutionary. Adding political, economical, and social examples helps students to organize their study of the American Revolution and to develop their answer to the question.

The various models provide the structure that makes the questioning work. Our attention turns to the three IBL models.

THE UNDERSTANDING BY DESIGN™ BACKWARD DESIGN MODEL

The UbD framework is a larger construct of teaching and learning into which inquiry fits. There are three stages: identify desired results, determine assessment evidence, and plan learning experiences and instruction. UbD uses the unit as the construct of teaching and learning. For our purposes, two important aspects draw our attention.

First, the entire UbD framework is inquiry-based since it revolves around asking and answering questions about various facets of teaching and learning. Each stage is organized around a set of key questions. For example, stage 1 has four questions, beginning with "What should students know and be able to do?"[15]

Second, a combination of long-term goals and essential questions prioritize what will be learned. The focus is on the transfer of learning so the goals generally describe what students will be able to do. In history, sample goals could include this: "Apply lessons of the past (historical patterns) to current and future events and issues and critically appraise historical claims."[16]

Each goal is paired with an essential question that activates learning to meet that goal. Essential questions come in two categories: general or overarching and topical. General or overarching essential questions apply to a larger context of a course. An example might be "How and why has war affected the development of the United States?" Topical questions are more focused, such as "How and why did World War II impact everyday life?"

Another important consideration is that the Understanding by Design™ Framework has influenced almost every other inquiry model that has been developed. The C3 Framework Inquiry Arc/Inquiry Design Model is a good example of that influence.

THE C3 INQUIRY ARC

To provide context, remember that the arc is part of the larger C3 goal to provide states with guidance in developing standards in civics, economics, geography, and history. The history components stress chronological reasoning focusing on

- change, continuity, and context;
- perspectives;
- historical sources and evidence; and
- causation and argumentation.

The Inquiry Arc is the "organizing structure" of the C3 Framework, focusing on "the nature of inquiry in general and the pursuit of knowledge through questions in particular."[17] The Inquiry Arc has four dimensions.

Developing Questions and Planning Inquiries

This dimension is the starting point of inquiry. Of most importance is the questioning. There are two categories of queries. Compelling questions frame the inquiry. Supporting questions are more detailed and focused. They help students gain information and develop understanding to answer the compelling question. The C3 Framework gives the following example of the two types of questions:

1. Compelling question: "Was the American Revolution revolutionary?"
2. Supporting question: "What were the regulations imposed on the colonists under the Townshend Acts?"[18]

The posing of questions starts the Inquiry Arc, leading to the second dimension.

Applying Disciplinary Concepts and Tools

This task asks students to apply historical methods and habits of mind to inquire into the topic. The questions, especially the supporting queries, guide the inquiry. Chronological reasoning is activated. Students answer basic *who*, *what*, *where*, and *when* questions before moving on to the *how* and *why*.

Students access and manage information from a variety of diverse sources to examine causality, make connections, evaluate significance, and set up the context. The goal is to come up with a plausible explanation based on logical interpretations of historical developments or events supported by relevant evidence. The phrase "relevant evidence" points out the key role played by the third dimension.

Evaluating Sources and Using Evidence

This section discusses the skills needed to access and analyze information as well as how to use what was learned to make conclusions. For Grades 6–12, gathering and evaluating sources involves accessing information from a number of sources guided by certain criteria. The distinction between middle and high school is that high school students examine sources reflecting a range of views while middle schoolers do not. An important task is evaluating the credibility of the source. Developing claims and using evidence involves identifying pertinent information and developing claims and counterclaims that evidence supports.

Communicating Conclusions and Taking Informed Action

The Inquiry Arc's innovative component is the last one that calls for taking civic action. It meets the overall goal of social studies to educate competent citizens who will be actively engaged in civic life in their classrooms, schools, and communities. Students have several action options, including the following:

- making decisions related to their classroom
- founding a school student organization or assuming a leadership position in an existing organization
- conducting research on an issue related to their community and presenting their findings to the public

THE INQUIRY DESIGN MODEL

While the C3 Framework laid out the Inquiry Arc process, apparently more description was needed resulting in the Inquiry Design Model publications, among other things.[19] The Inquiry Design Model has three phases: framing, filling, and finishing the inquiry. Each phase has several steps. As the title suggests, *Blueprinting an Inquiry-Based Curriculum* features plans or designs that describe different types of inquiry. The actual development of the nuts and bolts of the learning experience, possibly including goals, sequencing learning over weeks and days, and so forth, is left to the individual teacher.

Summary

Both UbD and the C3 Framework Inquiry Arc played major roles in inquiry-based learning becoming the dominant method in history education. They apply generally accepted concepts of effective inquiry-based learning in history, employing a skills-based approach to teaching and learning based on backward design. Both stress the idea of an essential or compelling question to guide the inquiry process. Most importantly, students are in charge of their learning. They conduct investigations by accessing sources, managing information, developing conclusions supported by evidence, and communicating their findings.

But UbD and the C3 Framework Inquiry Arc are not the only inquiry models being used in history classrooms. Variations of both as well as other strategies have been developed by teachers to meet the individual needs of their students. For over 20 years, the author of this book has been using an inquiry-based learning model developed independently to teach history and for use in social studies methods courses. We discuss that model in the next section.

INQUIRY-BASED PLANNING

Adapted over the years to accommodate new ideas and to better meet needs of preservice teachers, inquiry-based planning is predicated on the idea that practice makes perfect. It is a skill-based strategy. The teacher sets up a structure that is used for the unit, the week, the day, and the activity within a daily lesson. In each instance, there is a clear beginning, middle, and end to the learning experience. The structure builds a routine so that the teacher knows what to do when planning instruction and the students know what they will be doing when they enter the classroom.

Equally important, a pattern of learning adapted from the spiral curriculum concept is established. In 1960, Jerome Bruner presented his spiral curriculum design model.[20] The idea is that key concepts are studied regularly throughout a course of study with greater complexity or in differing applications. The inquiry planning model adapts Bruner's idea so that students meet content and practice skills multiple times in varied ways within a specific learning experience. The repetition of the process provides the practice needed to deepen content understanding while building skills at higher levels over time.

Before explaining how the model works, let's take a look at it. Figure 1.1 depicts the inquiry-based planning model for a middle school unit in U.S. history on European colonization. In this example, the major focus is on British colonization. If the unit were taught in Louisiana, the focus might include the French. In the southwest and California, it could be the Spanish.

Note that the model uses the C3 Framework terminology of the compelling question and that it has supporting questions to guide the teaching and learning of each week in a unit. It also features formative and summative assessments. Also, as is true for UbD and the C3 inquiry models, repetition and practice over time help students become more familiar with terms and

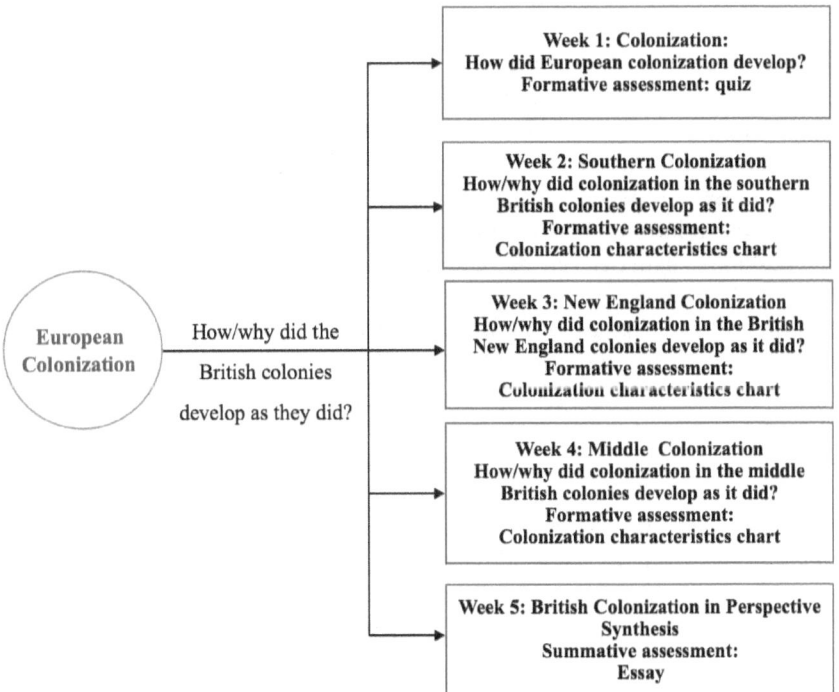

Figure 1.1. European Colonization. *Created by author.*

more expert with the process. As they become more proficient, students can apply the model with less teacher support and more independence.

As shown in Figure 1.1, a topic, question, and assessment are the major components of the model. The unit includes the general topic of study, the compelling question, and the summative assessment. A similar structure is used for the weekly subtopics. Each week is considered a somewhat distinct learning experience that connects to the overall unit. It consists of a subtopic, a supporting question that acts as the compelling question for the week, and a formative assessment. The last week assessment is the summative for the unit. If we were to move to the daily lesson, it would be organized around a topic, question, and formative assessment.

The unit and the week follow the same structure of a clear beginning, middle, and end. In the unit, week 1 serves as the introduction. Students are oriented to the unit topic, compelling question, and summative assessment. They also gain a big picture overview of the content topic, the proverbial survey of important people, places, and events. A sample assessment might be a quiz to ensure students have working knowledge of those people, places, and events. Weeks 2 and 3 are subtopic case studies that allow for more in-depth learning. Week 4 concludes the unit. Students synthesize what they have learned and complete the summative assessment.

Each week and each day repeat the beginning, middle, and end structure. Day 1, typically but not necessarily Monday, introduces the weekly subtopic, question, and possibly the formative assessment for the week. It also features a hook to interest students in studying the subtopic and access their prior content knowledge. During Days 2–4, students explore the topic in varied ways. Day 5 closes the week's learning with a formative assessment. Each daily lesson has an introduction, exploration, and conclusion.

Substantial benefits can be reaped by employing the same structure for the unit, the week, and the day. A routine is established that extends across the school year. The teacher knows how to plan for each unit and each day. The student know that each Monday will introduce a topic. Each Friday will close the study of the topic (or perhaps be a transition to the following week). In-between they will explore the topic. The specter of tedium is reduced because the content changes and the activities are adapted over time to address increased student proficiency.

Equally important, students meet the content and practice skills multiple times at each level of learning: unit, week, and day. The continued engagement helps students improve their content knowledge and skills mastery. Depending upon student proficiency, teachers can introduce more complex content and tasks. They also can reduce their presence in the classroom, so students gain more responsibility and control over their learning.

It bears repeating that every inquiry model has a similar trajectory. They all provide a pattern of learning that is to be applied over time at progressive levels of difficulty as students demonstrate proficiency. The differences are in the details of the respective inquiry models.

Yet another similarity among all inquiry models is that while they promise to improve teaching and learning, they also pose some serious challenges. To reap the rewards inquiry can bring, the challenges need to be overcome.

Inquiry-Based Learning Promises and Challenges

As is true of any method, inquiry-based learning has benefits and drawbacks. If we just pay attention to the rewards, embracing inquiry-based learning seems a no-brainer. If we look beyond those rewards to what it takes to earn them, a different story emerges. We will start with the benefits and then move to the challenges.

Already noted above, some of the benefits of IBL include more active student engagement and greater control over their education. Students are more motivated to learn. The greater engagement and higher motivation lead to increased proficiency. The gains in student learning benefit teachers who see a much better return from their investment in preparing learning experiences.[21] In addition, IBL provides a consistent strategy that is applied over time, meaning basic planning is reduced. The teacher can concentrate on helping students achieve higher levels of content understanding and skills competency.

The flip side is that IBL is not necessarily easy for teachers or students to master. If the teacher and students are new to inquiry-based learning, they likely will experience a steep learning curve as they seek to master the process. Patience and persistence are needed as mistakes will occur and failure at certain points is possible.[22]

IBL is time-consuming. For teachers, developing inquiry requires significant upfront planning and possibly more time spent to adapt the model to better meet student needs. Students also need substantial time to learn the IBL process, cutting into the finite time available in the classroom.[23]

CONCLUSION

Inquiry-based learning provides the method, the how, of effective teaching and learning of history. Mastering inquiry involves learning curves for teachers and students. Achieving that mastery requires patience and persistence. Most of all, though, it requires ongoing practice over time.

Inquiry is one-third of an effective trifecta of teaching and learning history. Primary sources and literacy comprise the other two thirds. They are discussed in the following two chapters.

NOTES

1. Eva Marie Kane, "Urban Student Motivation through Inquiry-Based Learning," *Journal of Studies in Education* 3, no. 1 (February 13, 2013):155–168; Joseph J. Gonzalez, "My Journey with Inquiry-Based Learning," *Journal on Excellence in College Teaching* 24, no. 2: 33–50.

2. Alison, "Teaching Critical Thinking Creatively," *Peacefield History*, n.d., https://peacefieldhistory.com/inquiry-based-learning-teaching/.

3. Alison, "Teaching Critical Thinking Creatively."

4. Erin, "How to Create Inquiry-Based Learning in Social Studies," *Let's Cultivate Greatness: Social Studies Resources That Empower*, n.d., https://letscultivategreatness.com/how-to-create-inquiry-based-learning-in-social-studies/.

5. Cited in Mary Sheldon Barnes (ed.), *Autobiography of Edward Austin Sheldon* (New York: Ives-Butler Company, 1911), 216–217.

6. National Council for the Social Studies (NCSS), *The College, Career, and Civic Life (C3) Framework for Social Studies State Standards: Guidance for Enhancing the Rigor of K–12 Civics, Economics, Geography, and History* (Silver Spring, MD: NCSS, 2013).

7. Florida State Board of Education, Florida's State Academic Standards—Social Studies, 2023 (Tallahasse, Florida: Forida State Board of Education, 2023), https://www.fldoe.org/core/fileparse.php/20653/urlt/6-4.pdf.

8. Brett L. M. Levy, Ebony Elizabeth Thomas, Kathryn Drago, and Lesley A. Rex, "Examining Studies of Inquiry-Based Learning in Three Fields of Education: Sparking Generative Conversation," *Journal of Teacher Education* 64, no. 5 (July 23, 2013): 388. DOI: 10.1177/0022487113496430.

9. Michiel Voet and Bram DeWever, "History Teachers' Knowledge of Inquiry Methods: An Analysis of Cognitive Processes Used During a Historical Inquiry," *Journal of Teacher Education* 68, no. 3 (2017): 314–318. DOI: 10.1177/0022487117697637. See also Levy et al., "Examining Studies of Inquiry-Based Learning in Three Fields of Education," 393–397.

10. Jay McTighe and Andrew Wiggins, *Understanding by Design Framework* (Alexandria, VA: ASCD, 2012), 2. This publication is a white paper summary of UbD: https://files.ascd.org/staticfiles/ascd/pdf/siteASCD/publications/UbD_WhitePaper0312.pdf, pp. 3, 7.

11. S. G. Grant, "From Inquiry Arc to Instructional Practice: The Potential of the C3 Framework," *Social Education* 77, no. 60 (November–December 2013): 325; Kathy Swan, John Lee, and S. G. Grant, *Inquiry Design Model: Building Inquiries in Social Studies* (Washington, DC: NCSS and C3 Teacher, 2018); Kathy Swan, John Lee, and S. G. Grant, *Blueprinting an Inquiry-Based Curriculum: Planning with the Inquiry Design Model* (Washington, DC: NCSS and C3 Teacher, 2019).

12. McTighe and Wiggins, *Understanding by Design Framework*, 3.
13. S. G. Grant, "From Inquiry Arc to Instructional Practice," 325.
14. S. G. Grant, "From Inquiry Arc to Instructional Practice," 325.
15. McTighe and Wiggins, *Understanding by Design Framework*, 3.
16. McTighe and Wiggins, *Understanding by Design Framework*, 3.
17. National Council for the Social Studies (NCSS), *The College, Career, and Civic Life (C3) Framework*, 46–49.
18. National Council for the Social Studies (NCSS), *The College, Career, and Civic Life (C3) Framework*, p. 12.
19. Swan, Lee, and Grant, *Inquiry Design Model*; Swan, Lee, and Grant, *Blueprinting an Inquiry-Based Curriculum.*
20. Jerome Bruner, *The Process of Education* (Cambridge, MA: Harvard University Press, 1960).
21. Kane, "Urban Student Motivation through Inquiry-Based Learning"; Gonzalez, "My Journey with Inquiry-Based Learning."
22. Gonzalez, "My Journey with Inquiry-Based Learning."
23. One reason teachers do not use inquiry relates to time. Barton, Keith and Linda Levstik, "Why Don't More History Teachers Engage Students in Interpretation?" *Social Education* 61, no. 6 (2003): 358–361.

Chapter 2

Primary Sources

At the beginning of the school year, in a U.S. history classroom, a teacher wanted to make sure students knew what a primary source was. The teacher asked students what they knew about primary sources, getting vague answers about being original sources and not being textbooks. Most students commented that they were confused about the distinctions between primary, secondary, and other sources. In response, the teacher designed an exercise to answer a simple question: What is a primary source?

Students examined two different documents on Thanksgiving, identifying the title, the creator, the date of creation, the place of creation, and the type of document:

1. Edward Winslow letter excerpt, December 11, 1621
2. A painting of the first Thanksgiving created in 1914 (Figure 2.1)

Students analyzed the Edward Winslow letter excerpt below:

> Our harvest being gotten in, our governor sent four men on fowling, that so we might after a more special manner rejoice together, after we had gathered the fruit of our labors; they four in one day killed as much fowl, as with a little help beside, served the company almost a week, at which time amongst other recreations, we exercised our arms, many of the Indians coming amongst us, and among the rest their greatest King Massasoit, with some ninety men, whom for three days we entertained and feasted, and they went out and killed five deer, which they brought to the plantation and bestowed on our governor, and upon the captain, and others. And although it be not always so plentiful, as it was at this time with us, yet by the goodness of God, we are so far from want, that we often wish you partakers of our plenty. We have found the Indians very faithful in their covenant of peace with us.[1]

Edward Winslow was identified as the writer. A quick Internet search by students confirmed that Winslow was an original Plymouth settler. They also confirmed that the letter was written soon after the meeting between the English colonists and the Wampanoags occurred. Using that information, students identified a primary source as a document created by an eyewitness who was present at the time and place of the event being described. The students expanded the definition to include physical artifacts and possibly any other type of sources, adding firsthand to apply to artifacts and other physical sources.

Next they analyzed a 1914 painting depicting the first Thanksgiving (Figure 2.1 below).[2] Students quickly recognized that the painting was not created at the time the scene depicted occurred. The teacher asked, "Is the painting a primary source?" The students analyzed the painting and its bibliography, commenting that Jennie August Brownscombe painted *The First Thanksgiving at Plymouth* in 1914, over 190 years after the event. From the perspective of Brownscombe not being a firsthand eyewitness at the place and time of the first Thanksgiving, the painting was not a primary source.

The teacher suggested they probe deeper into the concept of a primary source. The teacher agreed that the painting was not a primary source in the sense of being a firsthand eyewitness of the first Thanksgiving in Plymouth. But, the teacher asked the students if the painting looked like what they pictured the first Thanksgiving to be. Many agreed it did.

The teacher asked if the painting could be considered a primary source of how people at a later time, 1914 for example, perceived an event. The students seemed uncertain. The teacher asked what qualities largely defined a primary source. The students discussed the question and came up with four basic terms: firsthand, eyewitness, time, and place. The document has to be

Figure 2.1. Thanksgiving. Jennie August Brownscombe. The First Thanksgiving at Plymouth. *Wikimedia Commons (1914).*

a firsthand physical object or a written, visual, or other type of account created by an eyewitness at that specific time and place. Using those criteria, the students agreed that the painting could be a primary source, not regarding the first Thanksgiving but showing how people in 1914 pictured it.

Based on the definition they devised, students evaluated other types of sources. Textbooks, online encyclopedias, and information sites such as Wikipedia were normally not primary sources. To conclude the discussion and assess if students understood what a primary source was, the teacher asked, "What if you are studying how textbooks depict a people or culture, or a past event, such as Thanksgiving? The students agreed in that context, the textbook was a primary source. It fit the criteria of being firsthand at the time and place because it was the focus of study.

OVERVIEW

This chapter explores the world of primary sources. The discussion focuses on answering the following questions:

1. What is the value of primary sources as educational resources?
2. Why is it important to understand the nature of primary sources?
3. What are the various types of primary sources?

An underlying query is this: What has been the impact of technology on primary sources?

THE VALUE OF PRIMARY SOURCES

Over time, the value of using primary sources in the classroom has been often noted. Primary sources motivate learning. They bring students closer to the people, places, and events being studied so they can step into the place and time to better understand the people being studied. Primary sources pique the curiosity and interest of students, sparking inquiry. Studying primary sources improves student content understanding while building skills. Put simply, primary sources make students think critically about what they are studying. To reap the benefits of using primary sources, teachers must understand how they work and that requires exploring their nature.

THE NATURE OF PRIMARY SOURCES

For teachers and students to use primary sources effectively as historical resources, the starting point is understanding that each and every primary source is subjective and incomplete by nature. Whether it be a letter, government document, photograph, painting, physical artifact, or any other type, the primary source tells an incomplete story from a certain perspective. Each primary source represents one piece in a larger puzzle. If students only study a single primary source, they get a skewed, deficient version of a person, event, and so on. When they explore multiple primary sources that have different perspectives, they gain more full-bodied understanding.

For example, Winslow's purpose in writing the letter was to inform his friend truthfully about life in Plymouth. The excerpt describing the first Thanksgiving at Plymouth presents his version of events from the English perspective. Winslow highlights the bountiful harvest and the Wampanoag coming to the settlement where they joined the English colonists in a three-day feast, contributing five deer to the celebration.

As is true generally of a single primary source document, the letter generates more questions than it answers. Why did the Wampanoags come to Plymouth? Why did they kill five deer and gift them to the English? What does Winslow mean when he writes that food was not always plentiful? What happened before the meeting? What happened afterward?

The Winslow letter excerpt shows how study of a single primary source can propel the inquiry process. The questions raised by the letter lead students to study more documents that answer some questions while raising others. As the process continues, student knowledge grows and their skills are honed.

What would students learn by answering the above questions? They would gain new understanding of the meeting of peoples in New England and a more realistic view of what is called the first Thanksgiving. Unlike the traditional storyline, it was not a planned event, and the English were not thanking the Wampanoags for their help. The Wampanoags heard much gunfire and came to Plymouth to help the English because they thought the community might be under attack. As for the celebration, it was an exercise in diplomacy that resulted in a political alliance between the two groups that lasted 50 years.[3]

The examination of the Winslow letter shows how a single primary source can spark inquiry that promotes student learning. How effective that learning is depends upon teacher and students understanding not just what primary sources are; they also need to know how primary sources work. Primary sources are not just historical documents, they also are communication media. By examining primary sources as media, further insight is gained into their subjective, incomplete nature. In addition, viewing primary sources as media opens opportunities for their use in the history classroom.

Primary Sources as Media

Every primary source is created to send a message to a specific audience or audiences, though they are often received by unintended audiences, too. Initially, the message is for a contemporary individual, group, or the public. Originally, Winslow's letter was sent to a friend. As a historical primary source, the message is for scholars, teachers, students, or other interested people at later times and different places.

To receive the message, teachers and students ask questions that open up a dialogue with the source. As a result, primary sources act as channels of communication, as media that transmit and deliver messages. By perceiving primary sources as media, teachers and students can explore the role the communication process plays in the creation, distribution, reception, and effect of the primary source's message. The communication process has several components. Each has its own perspective that contributes to the nature of primary sources. Using perspective to explore primary sources provides insight into why they are subjective and incomplete.

Berger traced the concept of perspective back to European Renaissance art. He suggested that perspective in art centers everything on "the eye of the beholder," and that it "makes the seeing eye the centre [Berger's spelling] of the visible world."[4] Perspective can be described as a well-defined, focused frame of reference or point of view. The process of defining and focusing determines what is and what is not included. Perspective also influences how well the intended message is received and its effect.

Lasswell's Adapted Model of Communication

Describing primary sources as media emphasizes how they function. An adapted version of a basic model of communication political scientist Harold Lasswell developed in 1948 can help examine primary sources.

Lasswell's model divides the communication process into components in a succinctly phrased single question: Who says what in which channel of communication to whom with what effect.[5] The model explores the process of creating, sending, and receiving a message as shown by the following description of its components (noted in parentheses). For some purpose, the creator of the source (*who*) wants to send a certain message (*what*) using a specific medium (*channel of communication*) to transmit that message. It is received by various audiences, intended or not (*whom*) eliciting some sort of response or not (*effect*).

Lasswell focused on the time when the message was originally sent. The model has been adapted for studying primary sources to accommodate the reception and effect of the message over time. The adaptation also recognizes that the message can be received in different places either at the time of publication or later.

Figure 2.2 below examines Lasswell's adapted model emphasizing the varying perspectives of each component. It identifies the model's components regarding the creation, dissemination, reception, and effect of primary

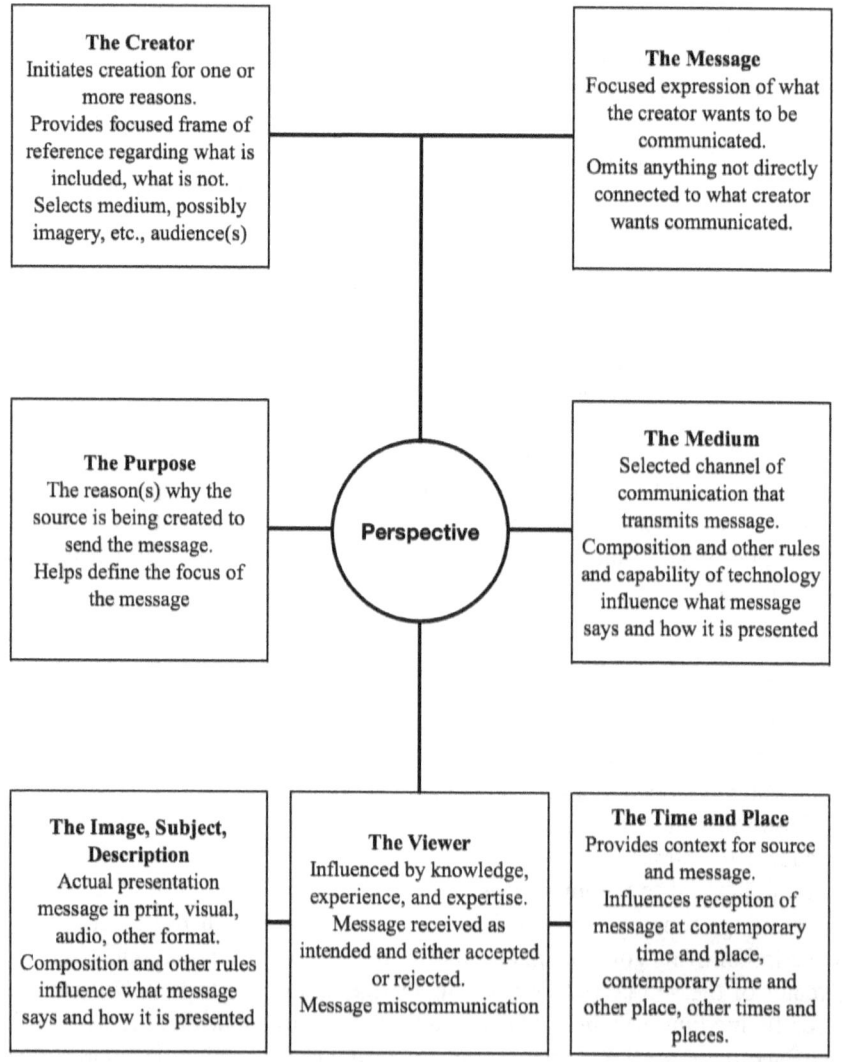

Figure 2.2. Perspective. *Created by author.*

sources over time and place. The chart briefly describes each component's perspective. Individually and together the various perspectives impart subjectivity and incompleteness to primary sources. Each component is directly connected to the message, helping shape what is said; how it is conveyed, disseminated, and received; and its impact on various audiences.

If students were examining a primary source, they could use Lasswell's adapted model to answer some basic questions to help them explore the source. Students can probe into the creation, dissemination, and reception of a primary source. They also could assess its effect at the time and place, at other places, and at other times.

While applying the entire model is possible, teachers can select what components students focus on to examine a primary source. Teachers also can be creative when designing primary source activities, using the model as a guide. For example, in his letter, Edward Winslow (*who*) described the first Thanksgiving in Plymouth (*what*) in a personal letter (*channel of communication*) to an old friend (*whom*). We do not know the immediate effect but the later effect was helping historians clarify the circumstances that led to the first Thanksgiving in Plymouth.

Students could then probe deeper into all or some of the model components, such as researching Edward Winslow and why he is important. They could research the details of the meeting between the Wampanoags and the English. No matter how the model is used, teachers and students need to know how the communication process works.

The Communication Process

Each component of the communication process has a distinct perspective. The primary source's original message reflects the creator's ideas, beliefs, knowledge, and attitudes, representing one side of a larger story. The people receiving and/or responding to the message do so based on their own attitudes, beliefs, and knowledge.

As a result, a message is typically neither objective nor complete. Instead, it tells the creator's version of the message influenced by the medium. Another important consideration is whether the original message is received as intended. In addition, as the painting exercise indicated, time and place play important roles. How was the message received in different places at the time of publication? How was the message received at later times?

Applying Lasswell's adapted model to study the various perspectives of primary sources provides opportunities for effective history teaching and learning. To a certain extent, taking advantage of the opportunities primary source analysis offers depends upon the teacher and student knowing about the various types of sources.

TYPES OF PRIMARY SOURCES

In the world of primary sources, a firsthand eyewitness implies being there. A wide variety of media, artifacts, structures, and aspects of the natural environment are primary sources if they meet the time and place criteria. The different types can provide students with unique opportunities to explore a topic from varying perspectives. As they study diverse primary sources, students gain a full-bodied picture of a person, place, event, or movement while developing important skills. They read, they see, and they may even touch, smell, or taste primary sources.

For example, in studying a battle, students could consult a map, photographs and drawings, film/videos of those fighting, and examine visuals or artifacts of weaponry. They could study before and after pictures of the battlefield. They could read personal accounts from both sides of the battle.

Or, when investigating a reform effort, such as woman suffrage, improving working conditions, or securing civil rights, students could explore an array of different types of primary sources. They could examine laws, pictures of marches and other protests, fliers and posters, blogs and social media postings, letters and diaries or memoirs, and so on.

Equally important, each primary source has type-specific characteristics. Whether it be a photograph, a map, or a written document, among others, each medium has unique characteristics that influence how the message is communicated. The structure and composition, the physical and possibly technological attributes determine how the message looks and what it can or cannot include. A business letter follows different composition rules than a personal letter does. A tweet is confined to a certain number of characters, currently 280.

Similarly, the technology of the primary source's production and dissemination influences what the message looks like, how it is perceived, and how it is distributed.[6] A photograph is restricted by what the camera lens can capture as is a film/video.

Exploring the Types of Primary Sources

The world of primary sources is vast, encompassing virtually everything. The following discussion organizes primary sources into categories and subcategories. It describes each category and offers some ideas on using them in the classroom.

Print Documents

The most familiar type of primary source is probably the print document. As is true of other primary source categories, print documents encompass a huge array of resources that comprise the written historical record. Print documents can be grouped as being public or personal primary sources. The U.S. Declaration of Independence is one form of a public print primary source, a government document. The list below includes some but not all of the print primary sources. Note that many primary sources fit into more than one category.

Public documents include the following:

- government laws, reports, charters, treaties, court records, census and other statistics, presidential and other official papers, and other sundry paper and digital publications
- publications such as newspapers, magazines, histories, autobiographies, travel accounts, literature, and various electronic publications

Personal documents consist of the following:

- formal sources that include wills, contracts and other agreements, certificates and licenses, tax returns, emails, and financial statements
- informal documents such as diaries and memoirs, letters and post cards, emails, blogs, texts, social media posts, memoranda and notes, and family and household records

The vast array of print documents allows students to examine many aspects of public and personal life, including themselves and other families. Students might study their family and search public records for immigration and census data. They can also obtain personal records such as birth and death certificates, letters, and diaries. The combination of the public and private print documents helps them to create a rich family history that they can connect to various historical events and the like.

Visual Documents

Visual documents encompass the pictorial historical record. Here, too, a vast range of subtypes exist. Editorial cartoons, photographs, maps, paintings, graphic arts such as posters, and building and other plans are just some of the myriad types of visual primary sources.

Visual documents can be used separately or with other types in numerous ways. Exploring past and present photos and maps helps students see how communities have changed and also how some aspects have remained the same. Events can be visually reconstructed by consulting photos, drawings, maps, and other visuals of battles, celebrations, and rallies, among many others. The same is true of media documents described below.

Media Documents

To simplify matters, visual and media documents have been divided into two categories. One distinction is that visuals are static and media have motion. Other distinctions are media include electronic examples from other categories and audio. Media documents include the following:

- entertainment productions such as tv shows, feature films, and sports programming
- news clips and newscasts
- documentary films
- amateur home movies
- advertising productions such as commercials and infomercials
- social media and streaming video, such as Instagram, TikTok, and other similar apps
- audio media including radio programs, podcasts, webinars, and online forums

Oral Culture

Anything passed down by word of mouth is oral culture. Examples are legends and myths, fables and children's stories, epic tales such as the *Iliad* or *Odyssey*, music, audio recordings, and podcasts.

Oral culture adds an audio dimension to primary sources. Students not only read and see, they hear about people, place, and events. The audio recordings of interviews with ex-enslaved people conducted in the 1930s add a personal perspective to the study of slavery and the era after 1865. Listening to the British prime minister Winston Churchill talk about Great Britain during World War II or President Franklin D. Roosevelt discuss the Depression of the 1930s adds nuance to the study of those topics.

Material Culture

All artifacts of human construction comprise material culture. Clothing and shoes, tools and machinery, money, furniture, weapons, toys, games, cell phones, television sets, and a laundry list of other items are material culture primary sources. We can use artifacts such as arrowheads, axes, and pottery to trace migration and trade in societies.

Students can study tools and machinery to explore manufacturing, agricultural production techniques, and to explain why some cultures prefer one tool over another. For example, the plow was used to prepare the land for planting in some regions of the world, but the Chinese used the hoe. In areas where the topsoil was shallow and fragile, such as arid regions of Africa and North America, a stick created a hole for seed.

The Built Environment

Everything people have constructed can be a primary source. For example, statues are excellent primary sources that tell students a great deal about a society and its values, especially important people and events. What does the Statue of Liberty tell us about the United States? Buildings, bridges, roads, and other structures also are excellent sources for study.

Using the built environment as a primary source often combines learning outside and inside the classroom. Students get to see, touch, hear, and smell everyday life. Imagine walking across a bridge or actually visiting a building that played a role in history.

A walking tour of the school neighborhood, a downtown area, or even a shopping mall opens many opportunities to explore such themes as change and continuity and the impact of invention and technology, among other things. Students could explore old pictures of their community, comparing the pictures to what they saw during the walking tour to gauge how some things change while others remain the same.

The Natural Environment

Often overlooked, landforms, waterways, vegetation, and weather also are excellent primary sources. A major theme of geography and certainly prominent in history is the interaction of people with their natural environment. Studying the Nile River and the surrounding desert provides insight into why Egyptian civilization has always lived along a narrow strip of land near the river. By examining the soil, original vegetation, and climate of the Great Plains region of the United States, students can better understand how the natural environment and human interaction with it caused the Dust Bowl of the 1930s.

Most types of primary sources are accessible on the Internet. Technology has revolutionized the world of primary sources in many ways. Amid all the promises technology brings to primary sources, there are also many perils.

THE PROMISE AND PERIL OF TECHNOLOGY

The rise of the Internet and the digitization of primary sources helped transform teaching and learning history. Every day more primary sources become available to teachers and students. Before the Internet, access was difficult and limited to paper publications. Today, the Library of Congress, the Digital Public Library of America, the National Archives, History Matters, and Wikimedia, among others provide teachers with millions of documents. Often the documents are complemented with resources on using primary sources in the classroom. A big issue today is sifting through the massive amount of primary sources available.

Technology also provided other benefits. Digitization has improved the quality of many documents, making them easier to read. Teachers can archive primary sources on their computers for later use and often they can use apps to further improve quality. In many cases, it is possible to zoom in on details when exploring a map or other primary source online.

Conversely, technology has created issues regarding the authenticity and reliability of primary sources. There are websites that cannot be trusted to provide legitimate primary source documents for various reasons. Some are open to anyone uploading sources. Another issue is that some sites promote a specific agenda and may manipulate sources to fit that agenda. Digitization makes it easy to alter sources in a variety of ways that can lessen or eliminate their viability.

Teachers need to be careful regarding what sites they access and what primary sources they select. Google has a Transparency Report webpage you can consult to assess a site. Also look for sites that end in .edu or .gov as they tend to be reliable. Check for ads; websites with an ad designation may or may not be reliable.

CONCLUSION

The vast and deep array of primary source types available to teachers provide rich opportunities for effective teaching and learning. But caution must be taken in selecting sources and ensuring they are what they purport to be. When integrated into the inquiry process, they help deepen student understanding of the topics being studied, if students possess the literacy skills to pursue inquiry and engage the primary sources.

NOTES

1. Edward Winslow, Letter, December 11, 1621. Caleb Johnson's MayflowerHistory.com. http://mayflowerhistory.com/letter-winslow-1621.

2. Jennie August Brownscombe, *The First Thanksgiving at Plymouth*. Wikimedia Commons (1914).

3. See David J. Silverman, *This Land Is Their Land: The Wampanoag Indians, Plymouth Colony, and the Troubled History of Thanksgiving* (London: Bloomsbury Publishing, 2019) for a revised story of the encounter between the Plymouth colonists and the Wampanoag.

4. John Berger, *Ways of Seeing* (New York: Viking Adult, 1973), 18.

5. Harold Laswell, "The Structure and Function of Communication in Society," in W. Schramm and D. F. Roberts (eds.), *The Process and Effects of Mass Communication* (Urbana:University of Illinois Press, 1971), 84–99.

6. Harold Innis, *The Bias of Communication* (Toronto: University of Toronto Press, 1951); Harold Innis, *Empire and Communication*, second edition (Toronto: University of Toronto Press, 1972); Marshall McLuhan, *Understanding Media: The Extension of Man* (New York: McGraw-Hill, 1964).

Chapter 3

Literacy

Imagine a history classroom where the teacher introduces the inquiry method and provides students with a print primary source to explore. Students respond favorably but then hit a roadblock when they have difficulty reading the source. In history, reading print documents creates several challenges, including vocabulary, archaic style and grammar, and the dense quality of the content. Strategies to help students read documents include using graphic organizers and providing definitions for terms within the text or glossaries.

In some instances, teachers rewrite all or parts of the document using language at the student reading level. A prominent educational researcher in history education once asked about rewriting historical documents. The answer probably reflected the responses of other history educators. If students cannot read the original document using it in the original form is useless, a complete waste of time. Instead, provide both the original document so students can see what it looks like and the rewritten version that they can more easily read. The strategy is similar to providing something in a world language class accompanied by an English translation.

The above discussion just applies to reading print documents. It does not encompass the various visual and multimodal texts used in many history courses. Every type of primary source has the potential to improve learning but each also has challenges. Several factors have contributed to the issue of reading skills in history. As noted above, the texts themselves are an issue. Low reading skills in Grades 6–12 reflect lack of progress in earlier grades. The rapid growth of different media is another issue. Accommodating multilingual learners and students with special needs also presents challenges. And the COVID-19 pandemic wreaked havoc at all levels of schooling.

This chapter examines the third leg of the triad, literacy, the skills set that activates inquiry-based learning stressing primary source analysis. Especially in our increasingly visual times where various media are increasingly present and proliferating in everyday life and education, literacy has become literacies. This chapter focuses on reading, answering the following questions:

1. What is the state of reading in Grades 6–12 in the United States?
2. How has the concept of literacy changed over time into literacies?
3. How can the progressive stages in the reading process be used to improve student historical literacy skills?

THE STATE OF READING IN THE UNITED STATES

The most recent National Assessment of Educational Progress (NAEP) reading assessment provides insight into student reading skills. In 2022, NAEP released the results of its most recent reading results for Grades 4 and 8 for the 50 states, the District of Columbia, and the Department of Defense schools. The eighth-grade assessment included 111,300 students nationwide. They read literary and informational texts to answer selected response (multiple response, matching, grid, zone, and in-line choice) and constructed response (written answer) questions.[1]

In 33 states, reading scores declined in Grade 8 between 2019 and 2022. Eighteen states did not experience a significant change and only one, the Department of Defense schools, showed an increase. Eleven states experienced a lower decline than the national average.

Looking at the level of student performance provides more insight into the reading issue. NAEP has three levels of achievement: basic, proficient, and advanced. The 2022 reading scores for eighth grade were as follows:

- 32% below Basic, four points higher than in 2019 and three points higher than in 1998
- 39% performed at Basic, the same as 2019 but three points lower than 1998
- 26% performed at Proficient, three points below 2019 and two points below 1998
- 3% performed at Advanced, one point below 2019 and one point above 1998.

Race, ethnicity, and income were also factors in the scores. African American eighth graders scored on average 24 points lower than white students, a similar gap existed in 1998. Hispanic students scored 17 points lower than white students in 2022, narrowing the gap by 10 points since 1998. Students eligible for the National School Lunch Program scored 23 points lower than students who were not eligible, a gap similar to 1998.

Examining the NAEP reading results for eighth grade over time shows that little general progress has been made since 1998. Similar percentages occurred at all achievement levels. Delving deeper into the national statistics show that only Hispanic students have improved their scores. The implication is that most students enter high school with barely adequate reading skills. Almost three of four eighth graders enter high school with below basic (32%) or basic (39%) reading skills. Less than one-third have proficient (26%) or Advanced (3%) reading skills.

In 2019, NAEP assessed reading scores for 12th grade. They also showed a rather flat line over time, with minor decreases between 2019 and 2015. Approximately 27,000 twelfth-grade students participated in the 2019 reading assessment, Thirty percent of 12th graders scored below Basic in 2019 compared to 28% in 2015. Thirty-three percent scored Basic in 2019 compared to 35% in 2015. The scores for Proficient and Advanced were stable in 2015 and 2019 at 31% and 6%, respectively. The trend in 12th-grade reading ability showed a slight decline from 1992. Basic went from 80% in 1992 to 70% in 2019. Proficient declined from 49% in 1992 to 37% in 2019.[2]

Regarding race and ethnicity, declines were evident among groups, though some were minor. Students eligible for the National School Lunch Program experience a 2-point decline between 2015 and 2019. Students not eligible for the lunch program experienced a 2-point increase.

NAEP concluded that 37% of 12th graders were academically prepared for college. Almost one in three students did not achieve basic reading levels. An important result was that there was no significant change in the average score of informational text comprehension between 2015 and 2019.[3]

Behind the Achievement Levels

The NAEP 2022 reading assessment evaluated cognitive targets, the kinds of thinking connected to reading comprehension. Eighth-grade questions focused on

- locating and recalling information;
- integrating and interpreting to make inferences within and perhaps across texts;
- critiquing and evaluating to critically assess texts from different perspectives; and for overall quality.

Twelfth-grade questions for 2019 were broken down by achievement level:

- *Basic*: identifying meaning and form, making inferences and connections, developing interpretations, and making conclusions supported by evidence
- *Proficient*: locating and integrating information, sophisticated analysis, and supporting inferences, interrelations, and conclusions with evidence

- *Advanced*: analyzing meaning and form of a text, providing complete, precise, and explicit support for analyses, and reading across multiple texts.

The NAEP skills reflect those needed for historical study. The eighth-grade skills are similar to those of 12th grade but less defined and sophisticated. The building of eighth-grade reading skills provides a strong foundation for succeeding in high school. Unfortunately, the scores indicate that many eighth graders enter high school unprepared for reading at the high school level. At least one-third of 12th graders leave high school with below college readiness reading skills.

The Local Character of Literacy

While national scores provide a larger context of student reading ability, literacy skills are a local affair, not just by state or district, or even, perhaps, by school, but by classroom. Many factors contribute to the local character of literacy. The characteristics of the student population are most important. What are the student literacy skill levels? What accommodations are needed for multilingual learners, students with special needs, struggling readers, and students performing above grade level? Another factor is the vast expansion of the term literacy regarding what it means and the numerous types.

MULTIPLE LITERACIES

We no longer speak of literacy only in the singular. Instead, we have applied the concept of literacy to almost every aspect of life leading to the notion of literacies. The full extent of the transformation of literacy is beyond the scope of this book. The focus here will be on historical literacy, but first some context.

Over the last 120 years, the rapid growth of information and knowledge caused a major shift in our perceptions of literacy, what knowing means, and education. Literacy is not solely concerned with basic reading and writing for memorizing and repetition. The vast expansion of information and knowledge has changed the definition of knowing from memorizing and repeating information to finding and using it effectively in everyday life, work, and education. As a result, the definition of literacy has expanded to highlight thinking and communication skills, including critical reading and thinking, communicating effectively, and problem solving.

The growth and increasing pervasiveness of media has also contributed to literacy expansion. Not only are there more media types, but they are also ever-present in everyday life and in many history classrooms. And we have gained more knowledge about media and how they work, also affecting literacy. As discussed in Chapter 2, each medium has its own literacy. Media growth led to a corresponding proliferation of visual imagery that has made visual literacy much more important in school classrooms.

Another factor is the growing diversity of the student population and recognizing the need to take multilingualism and culture into account in educating students generally. Regarding literacy, cultural relevance plays an important role. Students tend to learn better when they see themselves and their culture in what they study. In history, relevance has increased importance, since, in the past, many peoples and cultures were poorly or not represented in what was studied.

As a result, students need to develop "the intellectual tools and learning strategies needed to acquire the knowledge that allows people to think productively about history," and other subjects.[4] When they possess a basic understanding of the subject area, they can pose meaningful questions to guide their studies. Since students better comprehend how they learn, they become lifelong learners.

HISTORICAL LITERACY

Disagreement exists over the meaning of historical literacy. Is it the close reading of a historical text or the development of historical consciousness regarding the connections between past and present? Is historical literacy the higher-order skills related to interpretation, making inferences, and using historical sources to craft arguments? The answer is yes and more to all of the above questions.

Historical literacy combines thought and action with both informing the other. It includes the skills associated with historical thinking (habits of mind and methods of practice) that inform a person's historical consciousness. Historical thinking provides a framework for investigation stressing change and continuity by using chronological reasoning to evaluate cause and effect. The skills provide the tools and strategies to pursue the investigation. The findings increase understanding of historical thinking and consciousness.

Historical Consciousness

The starting point is recognizing that without being historically conscious, the study of history can be difficult because teachers and students will not have a larger construct for their studies. Without that big picture, not only is it difficult for students to connect what they study to themselves and their times, assessing significance is problematic.

What is historical consciousness? Scholars define the term differently. Herbert Gutman suggested historical consciousness means how people thought about the past.[5] We can extend that idea to define it as having a certain awareness of the connections between the past, present, and future.

Delving deeper, historical consciousness involves understanding the interaction of people, places, and time in varied scenarios, including the following:

- the interaction of people in a single place during a certain time period or over time
- the interaction of people in varied places during a certain time period or over time
- the interaction of people with their environment during a certain time period or over time
- projecting past and present interactions of people, places, and time into the future

In all of these scenarios, students apply aspects of historical thinking and practice skills to improve their understanding and to make meaning of their studies.

Two present-day movements work against developing a viable historical consciousness by distorting the historical record. The first is the push for the master narrative that emphasizes progress and unity but downplays or omits negative aspects of the historical record and diversity. The master narrative has already been discussed in previous chapters. The second movement is presentism, projecting present-day attitudes and beliefs back on the past without considering the context of that time.

Exploring Historical Consciousness and Presentism in the Classroom

Classroom activities can improve student understanding of historical consciousness while making them aware of the dangers of presentism. An issue today concerns attitudes toward the Founding Fathers of the United States. Taking a presentism stance, certain groups view the Fathers from one perspective, albeit an important one. They condemn the Founding Fathers for enslaving Africans and condoning slavery without considering their other ideas and actions that helped build the new nation. Thomas Jefferson, in particular, has been strongly castigated for enslaving Africans, his belief that African were inferior, and his relations with Sally Hemings.

Evaluating Jefferson from one dimension based on present-day ideas and attitudes, no matter how egregious his behavior, thwarts building understanding of history and how it works. He should be judged holistically within his people, place, and time context. Having students determine whether the negatives outweigh the positives is an excellent exercise for a U.S. history class. Some examples include a debate, a trial simulation, or a simple exercise completing a positive and negative balance sheet. All involve students exercising historical literacy skills to explore how people interacted over time to build their historical consciousness.

Jefferson's attitudes regarding Africans and slavery as well as his actions strongly tilt the balance sheet to the negative side. Even in his times, Jefferson wins no awards for enslaving Africans, as that practice was roundly criticized during his lifetime leading to laws against slavery in the northern states. His belief in the inferiority of Africans reflected the views of many but not all Americans of European stock. His relationship with Sally Hemings has been noted by historians for 50 years. Rumors of the relationship surfaced during his presidency leading to criticisms by Federalists, including John Adams.[6]

The positive side of the balance sheet also has strong achievements. Jefferson articulated the modern version of human rights when he wrote the Declaration of Independence that later served as a foundational argument against slavery. Jefferson's original draft condemned the slave trade, but that statement was rejected. He also founded the University of Virginia that was a model for public universities in the United States. And, when the issue of the expansion of slavery arose in 1820, he recognized the threat expansion posed to the nation, calling it "a firebell in the night."[7]

Mixed reviews come from his famous Louisiana Purchase in 1803 that doubled the size of the United States. Critics saw it as another example where he contradicted his statements against a strong executive and central government but acted in the opposite by competing the purchase without congressional approval. Supporters praised the action for eliminating a European power from North America and expanding the nation's territory. And, of course, the indigenous peoples living on the land were not consulted.

Assessing Jefferson holistically within his people, place, and time context allows students to come to their own conclusion about his legacy. Most likely, students will see Jefferson less as a mythological figure than a flawed human being with strong negatives and impressive positives. No matter what their conclusion is, students will practice historical literacy skills to build historical consciousness.

HISTORICAL LITERACY READING SKILLS

Reading, thinking, and communicating encompass historical literacy skills. They are used to conceptualize an investigation or study, conduct research, manage and evaluate information, develop a thesis and marshal support for that thesis, and communicate findings supported by evidence. To facilitate discussion, some of the skills have been organized into two categories. Inquiry skills have been discussed in Chapter 1 and they extend across the spectrum of historical literacy. Our focus here is on progressive reading that involves the exercise of many of the inquiry skills but from a different perspective.

Students read for different purposes, at times depending on skill level. The discussion here examines a progressive reading skill model that starts with pre-reading as preparatory to actual reading of the document. Next comes reading for content as the lowest level followed by analysis, critical interpretation, and significance, the highest level. The ability to progress through the levels depends upon competency at the lower levels. For example, students need to be able to read for content before moving on to analysis, and so on up to significance.

To show how the progressive reading model works, we will examine a document through all the stages. Editorial cartoons are valuable primary sources and familiar resources in history courses. Figure 3.1: If You Are Good Enough for War You Are Good Enough to Vote offers insight into opinions on women's suffrage during World War I.[8] The 19th Amendment, passed in 1920, granted women the right to vote.

Pre-Reading

Pre-reading includes accessing prior knowledge, sourcing, and a survey of the document to pose questions to guide its reading. Teachers can adjust the order of the pre-reading tasks to fit their classroom situation. This stage provides students with some baseline knowledge and prepares them for reading the cartoon. The discussion here will introduce the three tasks starting with accessing prior knowledge before moving on to sourcing and the survey of the document.

Accessing Prior Knowledge

In Grades 6–12 history courses, accessing prior knowledge is an important part of the pre-reading process, especially for multilingual learners or students with special needs. Accessing prior knowledge implies questioning

Figure 3.1. If You Are Good Enough for War. Morris, "If you are good enough for war you are good enough to vote." *The Brooklyn Magazine* (November 10, 1917). Library of Congress Prints and Photographs Division, Washington, DC. https://hdl.loc.gov/loc.pnp/cph.3b23212.

students about what they already know about the content of the topic being studied. When using documents, it also involves what students already know about the medium of the document and their prior experience working with that medium, in this case, an editorial cartoon. Once the teacher has evidence of what students know and can do, and students have prepped themselves for further study, sourcing occurs.

How the pre-reading exercise proceeds depends upon when the document is introduced. If used as hook for a topic, then the teacher cannot assume students have prior knowledge. In fact, an important objective is to diagnose what students already know about the topic before studying it. If used while a topic is being studied, the objective may be to refresh student memory on what they are learning. If employed at the close of the study, the objective may be to assess student knowledge. In any scenario, an important question is asking students if they have ever seen the primary source document and in what capacity.

Assume students are studying the cartoon during instruction on World War I and that they have studied women's suffrage in a previous unit on Progressivism. Possible questions to probe prior knowledge include the following:

1. Have you seen this cartoon before? If you have seen the cartoon, where did you see it and what do you remember about it?
2. What type of visual is it? What do you know about this type of visual?
3. What do you know about any connections between World War I and the women's suffrage movement?

Note that the last question does not ask about prior knowledge of World War I or women's suffrage but any connection between the two topics. The above question acts as a prompt to probe deeper into prior knowledge about both topics if needed.

Sourcing

Sourcing authenticates a document by checking its provenance to ensure it is what it purports to be. The sourcing process involves identifying typical bibliographic information such as the title, creator, date and place of publication, and the publisher. In the digital age, the authentication process has expanded to evaluating the reliability of the website and whether the document has been manipulated to change its content. Teachers can verify the site, or they can have students perform that task. Often, the website contains valuable background information. In addition to authenticating the document, sourcing provides important people, place, and time context information.[9]

How students go about sourcing depends on their experience with the task and also what information they have at their disposal. If students are new to the task or have not shown proficiency, generally the teacher leads the process. As students gain confidence, experience, and demonstrate expertise, they can work in groups and over time independently. No matter how the sourcing is done, all students must have the same information so sharing findings is important. Often, the document itself and perhaps the website where it was accessed provide the needed information.

The title and the cartoonist are located at the top of the cartoon. Because the date is missing, the teacher can provide the needed information or ask students to do further research. The cartoon is housed on the Library of Congress website, a trusted primary source repository. After students access the document on the site, they learn that the *Brooklyn Magazine* published the cartoon on November 10, 1917. The Library of Congress description also offers more information about the cartoon that can be easily gathered when reading it. The suggestion here is to not have the students read the description.

Sourcing is an important first step in reading a document. Skipping this step or having students do it later in the pre-reading process could thwart learning. Students may make inaccurate assumptions on the document topic, who created it, and the date and place of publication. As a first step, sourcing provides important basic information needed for further study, preparing students to survey the document.

Regarding the cartoon, students know who created it, the title, and that it was published seven months after the United States entered the conflict. They have also learned that U.S. soldiers first saw military action at the battle of Verdun in October 1917. U.S. soldiers had only been in combat for about a month when the cartoon was published.

The next step is surveying the cartoon to give students a big picture of the document. The survey provides basic information that helps students pose questions for reading it. When the visual is simple such as the cartoon, this step segues into the reading for content component and will be discussed in the "Reading for Content" section below.

Reading the Cartoon

The progressive reading sequence has four levels. The teacher can ask students to read at one level or several levels depending upon competence, The levels also allow for differentiation to meet individual student needs. The questions used to read the cartoon depend upon the reading levels. They can apply to the entire reading process or be posed for each level as needed.

Reading for Content

The beginning reading stage involves identifying items in a document or text using the questions *who*, *what*, *when*, *where*, and sometimes *how* to guide the reading. It does not involve higher-level thinking skills that are characterized by answering a "why" question. Generally, reading for content has three objectives. After completing the tasks, student will be able to

1. describe important components of the cartoon (people, objects and other items, any action, the place, and the time);
2. categorize the information in a graphic organizer; and
3. create a summary description in a paragraph or some other format.

The cartoon shows two figures but provides no inkling of where they are, so the reading focus is on the figures. To facilitate their reading, students pose a few questions:

1. Who is in the cartoon?
2. What do they look like?
3. What are they doing?

The answers to the questions help the students identify the two figures: Uncle Sam representing public opinion and a nurse representing American womanhood. Uncle Sam is an older white man with a beard wearing a top hat, a suit jacket, a vest and tie with stars, and pants with stripes. He is much taller than the white woman who is dressed in a nurse's uniform with a red cross on her head scarf. Uncle Sam has his right arm around the woman's shoulders and is holding her hand with his left hand. He is looking down at her as she gazes up at him.

The potential graphic organizer is a concept map with a circle in the center and three radiating arms with space to write. In the circle, students write the title. One radiating arm is for Uncle Sam, another for the woman, and the third is labeled action or what they are doing. A line below the concept map is for the summary sentence that might read "Uncle Sam as public opinion tells a nurse as American womanhood she is good enough to vote." The summary also identifies the overt message of the cartoon.

The remaining reading stages probe deeper into the cartoon. While the picture seems quite simple, it is open to sophisticated analysis, interpretation, and assessment of significance.

Reading for Analysis

Beginning with reading for analysis, students start asking *why* questions. Analysis can focus on change and continuity, cause and effect, or some other historical theme or element. The cartoon caption signals a great change is suggested relating to cause and effect. Analysis questions might include these:

1. Why are white women being considered good enough to vote?
2. What was the motivation for supporting this change?
3. How might the proposed change effect the status of women? The U.S. political system? American society?

The answer to the first and second questions are similar but phrased differently. In both cases, the answer is that women contributed "enough" to the war effort to be given the right to vote. The image of the nurse is important as it indicates some women are working near the battle front. The last question asks students to make inferences on the effect of women voting.

By 1917, 12 states had granted women the right to vote. Another useful statistic is the number of women in the United States at that time. According to the 1920s' census, there were almost 31,500,000 million men of voting age in the United States and almost 29,500,000 women.[10]

Woman suffrage almost doubled the voting population, transforming the political life of the United States. Women gained full political citizenship rights that not only included voting but also much greater opportunities to run for elective office. Both political parties had to change their strategies and activities to include women. Suffrage also furthered the efforts by women to gain equal rights in other areas of society, though many initiatives did not succeed for years or decades, or not at all.

Reading for Critical Interpretation

Reading for critical interpretation moves beyond traditional analysis to examine other messages in documents. Critical interpretation has students apply critical visual literacy skills to explore aspects of power, authority, and oppression. Often overlooked is that the same skills allow students to examine resistance and liberation. An intriguing method for interpreting a text critically is to have students assume the personalities of historical figures, in this case, women actively involved in the suffrage movement.

The following questions delve deeper into the meaning of the cartoon:

1. Who comprises public opinion in the United States?
2. Who has the power and authority in American society to provide women the vote?
3. What does your answer suggest about the role of women in the campaign for women's suffrage?

Students using the above questions to examine the cartoon get a different read on its messaging. Public opinion is personified by a familiar symbol of the United States, an older white man with a beard wearing patriotic clothing.

The symbol does not reflect the American people. Missing are women, African Americans, Asian Americans, Mexican Americans, indigenous peoples, and younger people. The students may question whether Uncle Sam, as envisioned, is an appropriate symbol for the nation and public opinion.

Similarly, older white men are pictured as the only people with the power and authority to give women the right to vote. Even though students learned that women led the suffrage campaign for decades, the caption suggests their agency in those struggles was not a factor in the debate over the vote. Only their efforts in the war mattered and, even then, the focus was on service to the military as nurses rather than workers or other jobs they undertook.

Examining the woman leads to similar findings regarding race. The nurse is a white woman. During an age of segregation, that meant suffrage was restricted by race to white women.

Critical examination of the cartoon provides insight into the power structure of the nation and the relations between genders and races during World War I. Women occupy a secondary, dependent status to men, and it is only through the largesse of white men that white women can gain, not earn, the right to vote. A good way to show change over time would be to compare this cartoon with the We Can Do It! poster from World War II (Figure 3.2 below). A muscled, determined, and competent factory worker, Rosie declares, "We Can Do It!" There is no doubt about agency in the World War II poster, women have the power, at least temporarily.[11]

But here, too, the question of race emerges. Can only white women do it? How would Indigenous, African American, Asian American, or Mexican American women view the picture?

The reading for critical interpretation example stressed issues of white male power and authority related to gender and race relations pictured in the cartoon. Critical reading can take various perspectives depending upon the document and classroom needs. Is it possible that a critical reading of the woman nurse might reach a different conclusion? Standing straight, looking directly at Uncle Sam, the woman confident and competent tells him that women are good enough, not only for war but also for voting. Based on the obvious affection shown by Uncle Sam, public opinion agreed.

Reading for Significance

The various stages of reading texts climb Bloom's revised taxonomy. Each stage builds upon the one before it. Assessing significance is the highest level. To a great extent, historical scholarship and education revolve around significance: the why do we care question. Significance is multidimensional and applies across space and time. There is significance at the time and place

Figure 3.2. We Can Do It. *We Can Do It!* (ca. 1943), Library of Congress, Prints and Photographs Division, Washington, D.C. https://hdl.loc.gov/loc.wdl/wdl.2733.

of publication, at the time of publication in different places, and over time in various places, including where it was originally published.

Open to differing interpretations, the Uncle Sam and nurse cartoon was a potent image of support in 1917. The use of the Uncle Sam symbol was a shrewd move. Uncle Sam had been used earlier to motivate young men to volunteer for the military after the United States entered World War I. The women's suffrage cartoon capitalized on the earlier cartoon to show that women's contribution to the war effort earned them the right to vote. As such, the suffrage cartoon likely persuaded people to support the 19th Amendment.

During this period, a large-scale women's suffrage campaign was also being waged in Great Britain. Cartoons also were potent media used by British supporters and opponents of women's suffrage. The transatlantic campaigns had strong ties, so it is likely the Uncle Sam cartoon was well-known in Britain.

Gaining the vote was a turning point in women's history. Not only did it elevate their status as voters but over time, more women ran for office at every level. The cartoon connects to the widespread election of women to state legislatures, as governors, congressional representatives, candidates for president, and the current vice president of the United States. An interesting development was the creation of the League of Woman Voters, a highly influential political organization, in 1920 several months before the 19th Amendment was ratified.

Students today can explore the expansion of women's rights historically. Starting with the rights women enjoy today, they can trace progress back to the women's suffrage campaign. They also can assess how difficult it was to obtain these rights and to identify what else remains to be done. For example, the Equal Rights amendment to the Constitution was drafted in 1923 but was not passed by Congress until 1973. It has not yet been ratified.

HISTORICAL LITERACY AND PROGRESSIVE LEARNING

Historical literacy skills follow a progressive learning sequence teachers can use to their advantage in the classroom. Not only can they assess learning over time to help students move to a higher level of competency, they can differentiate learning to meet individual student needs. The progression of competency moves across stages but also within each stage.

Scaffolding defines the levels. Whether it be reading for content, analysis, critical interpretation, or significance, teacher facilitation starts out heavy and decreases as students demonstrate competency. The goal is to have students successfully proceed through a stage independently. Once they have shown expertise at one stage, they can move on to the next. Student prior knowledge and ability determine where they fit along the reading progression. Especially for struggling readers, multilingual learners, and students with special needs, a carefully plotted skills progression facilitates differentiation and improvement.

One strategy follows a three-part scaffolding progression. Depending upon need, students work as a whole class to read a text. When they demonstrate competency, they move to working in groups and ultimately to individual work. Organizing groups by different skills and possibly language levels allows students to learn from each other. For example, partnering a multilingual student with proficient English language skills with a student with limited English skills eases or eliminates language barriers to learning.

CONCLUSION

This chapter explored historical literacy, focusing on reading. The various stages of reading were examined showing that they followed a hierarchy of skills that climbed Bloom's revised taxonomy. Historical literacy is the tie that binds inquiry and primary sources, making the triad work. A student's ability to read, think, and communicate largely determines how well they learn. A carefully plotted progressive learning strategy maximizes learning potential.

The next chapter discusses a critical question: whose history do students study? It examines the important issues of cultural relevance and inclusion that motivate students to learn.

NOTES

1. The following discussion of the NAEP reading assessment is based on the U.S. Department of Education. Institute of Education Sciences, National Center for Education Statistics, National Assessment of Educational Progress (NAEP), *The Nation's Report Card: 2022 Reading Assessment*, https://nces.ed.gov/nationsreportcard/subject/publications/stt2022/pdf/2023010NP8.pdf.

2. U.S. Department of Education, Institute of Education Sciences, National Center for Education Statistics, National Assessment of Educational Progress (NAEP), *The Nation's Report Card: 2019 Reading Assessment*, https://www.nationsreportcard.gov/highlights/reading/2019/g12/.

3. U.S. Department of Education, Institute of Education Sciences, National Center for Education Statistics, National Assessment of Educational Progress (NAEP), *The Nation's Report Card: 2019 Reading Assessment*.

4. John D. Bransford, Ann L. Brown, and Rodney R. Cocking (eds.,) *How People Learn: Brain, Mind, Experience, and School*, expanded edition (Washington. DC: National Academy Press, 2000), 4–5.

5. Gutman cited in Peter Seixias (ed.), *Theorizing Historical Consciousness* (Toronto: University of Toronto Press, 2006), 8. See also John H. Bickford III, "Primary Elementary Students' Historical Literacy, Thinking, and Argumentation about

Helen Keller and Anne Sullivan," *The History Teacher* 51, no. 2 (February 2018): 275; Courtney Luckhardt, "Teaching Historical Literacy and Making World History Relevant in the Online Discussion," *The History Teacher* 47, no. 2 (February 2014): 188; Arja Virta, "Historical Literacy: Thinking, Reading, and Understanding History," *Tidskrift: Historical Literacy, Journal of Research in Teacher Education* 4 (2007): 14. Robert Thorp, "The Concept of Historical Consciousness as an Interpretive Frame for Historical Media," April 23, 2013, https://www.researchgate.net/publication/258210159_The_Concept_of_Historical_Consciousness_as_an_Interpretive_Frame_for_Historical_Media.

6. See Fawn M. Brodie, T*homas Jefferson: An Intimate Biography* (New York: W. W. Norton, 1974); and Annette Gordon-Reed, *Thomas Jefferson: An American Controversy* (Richmond, VA: University of Virginia Press, 1998).

7. Thomas Jefferson to John Homes, April 22, 1820. Founders Online, https://founders.archives.gov/documents/Jefferson/03-15-02-0518.

8. Morris, "If you are good enough for war you are good enough to vote." *The Brooklyn Magazine* (November 10, 1917), Library of Congress Prints and Photographs Division, Washington, DC. https://hdl.loc.gov/loc.pnp/cph.3b23212.

9. S. Wineburg, (1991). "Historical Problem Solving: A Study of the Cognitive Processes Used in the Evaluation of Documentary and Pictorial Evidence," *Journal of Educational Psychology* 83, no. 1 (1991): 73–87; S. Wineburg, D. Martin, and C. Monte-Sano, *Reading Like a Historian: Teaching Literacy in Middle and High School History Classrooms* (New York: Teacher's College Press, 2013); K. Kolander, "Primary Sources: Meaning, Reliability and Where To Find Them," Shapell.org, American History and Jewish History Blog, January 31, 2022. https://www.shapell.org/blog/primary-sources-meaning-reliability-where-to-find-them/?gclid=Cj0KCQjwhqaVBhCxARIsAHK1tiMmMQLimz3vYRrAj1Bmtca83EpqvpddpIWHG3eqsICZjRhYnTjADf0aAlY_EALw_wcB.

10. U.S. Bureau of the Census, Department of Commerce, *Fourteenth Census of the United States Taken in the Year 1920: Volume III Population: 1920*. (Washington, DC: Government Printing Office, 1922), 18.

11. *We Can Do It!* (ca. 1943), Library of Congress, Prints and Photographs Division, Washington, DC, https://hdl.loc.gov/loc.wdl/wdl.2733.

Chapter 4

Whose History?

Teaching history can be a challenge as students may find it difficult to relate to the past. Some ask, "Why should I learn about these dead people; they lived so long ago?" Others comment, "Ugh! Boring!" If students are not asking these questions or voicing them aloud, they might be thinking such thoughts. An important task for a history teacher is to make what seems irrelevant and boring more appealing. Learning needs to be relevant, inclusive, and have meaning for the students. They learn best when they understand how the past has influenced the present and can see themselves in what is being learned.

One approach is to connect student experiences today to those in the past. For example, in a middle school world history class, how could a teacher spark interest in the study of ancient civilizations? How about opening a unit on Mesopotamia with an activity on what it was like to go to school in Sumer approximately 4,000 years ago? The focus on the school experience of their ancient peers provides present-day students with a familiar everyday experience. A teaser might be the teacher suggesting that without schools in Sumer and other ancient civilizations, there might be no text messages, since these cultures invented writing.

After establishing the people, place, and time context for the unit, ask the students to read the excerpt below that was taken from 21 clay tablets and fragments recovered from Sumer.[1] They compare what they learned about Sumerian schools to their own educational experiences and then pose questions for further study of ancient Mesopotamia.

The clay tablets transcribe a question-and-answer conversation possibly between a teacher and a student who was studying to be a scribe. The italics attempt to fill in missing words. After reading the excerpt, students compare their day to that of the Sumerian student.

"Schoolboy, where did you go from earliest days?" "I went to school." "What did you do in school?" I *read* my tablet, ate my lunch, prepared my tablet, wrote it, finished it; then *my prepared lines were prepared for me* (and in) the afternoon, *my hand copies were prepared for me.* Upon the school's dismissal, I went home, entered the house, (there) was my father sitting.

I *spoke* to my father of *my hand copies*, then *read* the tablet to him, (and) my father was pleased; truly I *found favor with* my father. "I am thirsty, give me drink, I am hungry, give me bread, wash my feet, set up the bed, I want to go to sleep; wake me early in the morning, I must not be late, (or) my teacher will cane me." When I awoke early in the morning, I faced my mother, and said to her: "Give me my lunch, I want to go to school." My mother gave me two "rolls," I *left* her; my mother gave me two "rolls," I went to school.[2]

The excerpt humanizes the study of the ancient world by describing a typical school day in Sumer. The activity is relevant and inclusive. School provides a context that connects students across time and space. Learning about a Sumerian school can create empathy as present-day students relate to the ancient student as a peer.

Students also learn about the historical theme of change and continuity. Ask students in groups to create a Venn diagram comparing schools in Sumer to their experiences today. Some similarities include reading, writing, eating lunch, going home after school, and talking about their day—and possibly worrying about being tardy to school the next day. Differences include vast distinctions in technology and who went to school in Sumer versus today. One glaring difference students likely will point out is the line that speaks of being hit with a cane if tardy to school. Corporal punishment is illegal today but was acceptable in Sumer.

CHAPTER OVERVIEW

Relevance and inclusion are watchwords of history education today. The terms help answer the question this chapter explores: Whose history? It is the student's history. The chapter discusses why it is important to make history relevant and inclusive for all students by answering the following questions:

1. Why is assessing significance important in history education?
2. How do themes connect past and present?
3. Why are cultural relevance and inclusion important?

SO WHAT? WHY DO I CARE?

In several ways, the questions "So what?" and "Why do I care?" explain why relevance and inclusion are important. They also strike at the heart of historical study and education. "So what?" is an essential question in history, probing into the significance of what is being studied at the time and up to the present day. "Why do I care?" builds on the "So what?" query connecting the student to the past, at times in a personal way, showing why it is significant for them. Answering the two questions helps students understand how seemingly unrelated historical events, people, places, trends, or movements directly link to them or their families.

"So what?" and "Why do I care?" also help teachers plan units, lessons, and activities. The questions are basic components of the inquiry, primary sources, and literacy triad. The queries stimulate inquiry by providing insight into developing the compelling question. Analysis of primary sources brings students closer to the peoples, places, and events being studied. The sources can include the voices of people representative of student backgrounds who played roles in the events being studied. To open a dialogue with the primary sources created by those people, students develop literacy skills.

The questions also help teachers implement the strategies of connecting past and present and cultural relevance. Connecting past and present increases student understanding of how and why past people, places, and events have influenced conditions today and will shape them in the future. In the process, students evaluate historical significance generally and for themselves, developing high level cognitive skills that they can apply in formative and summative assessments.

The caring component guides teachers in developing culturally relevant and inclusive content for studying a topic. Wherever possible, the teacher ensures that students learn about peoples and cultures representative of the classroom population. Because they see how their cultures, and possibly their families, played roles in the historical process, students understand why they should care about history. In units closer to the present, they might connect the experiences of their family or possibly themselves to what happened.

CONNECTING PAST AND PRESENT

An issue history teachers face is that our society, our world, tends to be present and future oriented, often neglecting the past. In part, technology and popular culture, think Star Wars, have helped create that mind set. Connecting the past to the present helps students understand that today is a culmination of yesterdays that stretch back a few years, centuries, or millennia. Writing in Sumer directly influenced writing today. We are practicing the same skill just not on clay tablets with a reed stylus.

Similarly, by studying the past as prologue to the present, students recognize that what we do today influences the future. Basically, past, present, and future are a continuum, a coherent sequence that has personal and global implications. Given the present and future orientation that dominates today, a caution is not to engage in presentism, using present attitudes and beliefs to explain the past. Yes, we interpret the past from the present but doing so requires taking into account the situation at the time and place of study. We use present-day knowledge to examine the past on its terms.

THEMES AS CONNECTORS

How can connections be made between the past and the present? Themes provide an answer. For our purposes, themes are content concepts, academic skills, or social-emotional skills that extend across units in a course. Typically, themes create linkages across units. Viewed from one perspective, what students study in history occurs where a topic and a theme intersect.

As a result, when students study themes across a course, they become more familiar with content vocabulary and concepts. They practice skills to improve their competency. Students improve their ability to apply the themes in their study of history. Over time, that familiarity allows students to work independently on more complex aspects of the theme as it relates to the topic of study.

How many themes should there be? The answer depends upon the situation. The five social studies content areas (civics/political science, economics, geography, history, and social sciences) can be themes. Or a theme may be more expansive such as everyday life or technology. Including academic and social-emotional learning skills adds to the total. Generally, less is more but too few is not enough. Too many themes can be confusing and unwieldy. Too few might not meet student needs. A combination of content and skills works best. My preference is three content themes and one academic skills and one social emotional theme.

What are potential content, academic skills, and social-emotional skills themes in the teaching and learning of history? How can themes connect the past and the present to promote relevant, inclusive student learning?

Content Themes

The major content areas of social studies influence what themes are learned in history. We will use political here instead of civics. In each case, a theme is broken down into one more sub-themes. The following list identifies some of the many possible themes:

1. *Political*: systems, government, rights, laws, war, and peace
2. *Economics*: systems, making a living, exchange, resources, technology, globalization
3. *Geography*: five themes of location, place, region, movement, human environmental interaction
4. *History*: change and continuity, cause and effect
5. *Social sciences*: systems, class structure, social institutions, culture

Because the primary content area is history, its themes act as overarching connectors for other subject area themes. Change and continuity and cause and effect help create bonds across disciplinary themes. No matter what historical topic students are studying, they examine change and continuity and cause and effect.

As noted above, some themes are overarching, spanning several, and often all content areas. Both everyday life and technology encompass all content areas and their respective themes. The same is true for the quest for rights and human-environmental interaction, among others.

In world history, themes help students organize the immense amount of content to make it more manageable for substantive learning. For example, studying one civilization can be overwhelming for teachers and students. The task is more daunting when several civilizations are studied. The social studies themes of geography, history, economics, political systems, and social systems provide a structure to organize the information and to facilitate analysis.

One approach is to have students examine each civilization in the same way to gain an overview and for in-depth study. This provides students with a good working knowledge of a civilization. The working knowledge prepares them to delve more deeply into an aspect of that civilization.

Working with maps, timelines, biographies, and descriptions of important events provides students with a people, place, and time context for a civilization generally and regarding in-depth studies of specific aspects. Regarding the general overview of the civilization, the maps show where it developed initially and expanded or contracted over space. Maps also identify important geographic and human-made features and places. A timeline identifies important events and possibly people, chronologically charting the civilization's development over time. Brief biographies introduce important people while brief descriptions of important events or movements expand upon entries in the timeline.

Constructing a table expands the civilization database. Selected themes act as categories for the table. Whether for a general overview or for a specific case study topic, tables that include political, economic, social, and cultural characteristics provide a snapshot of what is being studied. Tables can provide an overview of the civilization or organize important aspects of a case study.

The maps, timelines, and so on serve several purposes. All combine learning content with developing academic content and literacy skills. If completed collaboratively, students build social-emotional skills.

Skills Themes

The two skills categories discussed here are academic and social-emotional. Academic content skills provide students with the ability to study content. Each subject area has specific skills related to that discipline. Historical inquiry skills were discussed in Chapter 1 and historical literacy skills in Chapter 3. Social-emotional skills relate to the overall development of the student. For students to improve their skills, they must practice them over time. Integrating the maps, timelines, bios, and table activities into the ongoing flow of teaching and learning throughout a unit and a course provides the needed practice.

Academic Content Skills

In history education for Grades 6–12, academic content skills are often developed within a multidisciplinary context. One subject area may be emphasized, but generally learning involves other subject area content and skills. Almost every history topic includes working with maps, timelines, and likely charts and tables that connect to skills in other social studies disciplines. In many cases, math and science content is integrated into learning, meaning skills in those subjects also are developed. Students may analyze population and other statistics, or they measure map components. The scientific method may be part of the inquiry process.

Regarding the social studies content areas, the list below provides some examples of skills in each discipline:

- economic reasoning: decision making on the use of economic resources
- geographic reasoning: spatial and environmental perspectives
- historical thinking: chronological reasoning, assessing cause and effect, and change and continuity

- social science (related to political science, sociology, anthropology and psychology): inductive and deductive reasoning; the scientific method; quantitative reasoning; decision making; and assessing social, cultural, and psychological contexts

Inquiry and literacy skills are foundations for the subject area content skills.

Social-Emotional Skills

According to the Collaborative for Academic, Social, and Emotional Learning (CASEL), social-emotional learning (SEL) skills relate to an individual's overall development. They help students "develop healthy identities, manage emotions and achieve personal and collective goals, feel and show empathy for others, establish and maintain supportive relationships, and make responsible and caring decisions."[3] CASEL identified five important SEL skills: self-awareness, self-management, responsible decision making, relationship skills, and social awareness.

Building social emotional skills follows similar guidelines to developing academic skills or improving content knowledge. It involves engaging students actively in their learning as well as practice over time to build skills. Classrooms that emphasize collaboration support the development of SEL skills.[4] Working in groups is one strategy that could be a theme that helps students build social-emotional skills.

THEMES IN PERSPECTIVE

While the above provided separate discussions on content and skills, they are inextricably connected in the classroom. Students learn the content by practicing skills. Content themes connect learning about the past to the present. The same theme that connects content horizontally across a course or unit can create a logical vertical sequence over time.

The activity on writing in Sumer focuses on a familiar part of everyday life, projecting it back in time and place and then bringing it up to the present. Students practiced literacy skills to learn the content and construct the Venn diagram. Their analysis of the content and of the Venn involved such content skills as chronological reasoning, cause and effect, change and continuity, and decision making. Working in groups developed SEL skills. As you read the following example on the social compact and rights, identify the various themes present in the activity.

The Social Compact and Rights

A foundation of human society is the creation and maintenance of a community. The idea of a social compact for a civil community or a covenant for a religious community dates back at least three thousand years. During the Enlightenment of the 17th and 18th centuries, the idea arose that humans were by nature free. Forming a community and a government to order that community required the voluntary consent of the people involved. The consent was called a social compact or contract.

In *The Social Contract*, eighteenth-century French philosopher Jean-Jacques Rousseau described the social compact concept. He suggested that the social contract (or compact) solved the issue of maintaining freedom while submitting to the needs of a community. All those joining the community agree to give up some individual freedoms in return for gaining the benefits of the community, equally enjoyed by all.[5] Being a community member means that while some freedom is surrendered, you gain certain rights. Community members also incur responsibilities. The ability to maintain those rights depends upon assuming those responsibilities.

Certain sections of the Declaration of Independence (Declaration) and the Preamble of the U.S. Constitution (Preamble) comprise the social compact of the United States. The Declaration's second paragraph lists certain inalienable rights including life, liberty, and the pursuit of happiness. The Declaration also states that the people had the right to change or end a government if those rights were violated, establishing a new government in its stead. The final paragraph proclaims independence and establishes the United States of America as a sovereign nation so its citizens can enjoy those rights.

The Preamble reiterated the proclamation of a new nation and established the Constitution as the law of the land. The Preamble also described the goals of the nation: "form a more perfect union, establish justice, insure domestic tranquility, provide for the common defense, and secure the blessings of liberty."[6] The first ten amendments to the Constitution, known as the Bill of Rights, further detail what rights citizens enjoy. Since 1892, in return for enjoying their rights, U.S. citizens have pledged allegiance to the republic at schools and at many public events. The pledge of allegiance confirms acceptance of the social compact of the United States.

Rights are a prominent concern of middle and high school students both in their public and personal lives. Studying the idea of a social compact and its relationship to rights improves student understanding of the dynamic quality of past actions over time. It also makes the past action real and important.

After studying the Declaration of Independence and the U.S. Constitution as components of the nation's social compact, ask students to explore their rights today. They also might examine a historical or recent controversy to see how that dispute connected to the nation's social compact. After studying the election of 2020 and subsequent events, students could assess whether the actions of certain people and groups violated the social compact and what the consequences should be. Students also could create a social compact for the classroom community.

Using themes to connect past events to the present day increases student understanding of the historical theme of change and continuity. In the process of learning they develop important skills. They also connect what is happening in their lives to the topic of study to answer the "So what?" and "Why do I care?" questions. A corollary to connecting past and present is ensuring that the history curriculum students study is inclusive and culturally relevant to them.

CULTURAL RELEVANCE

Where do I fit in? What is being learned? Where does my culture fit? These questions demonstrate the need for cultural relevance. If students do not see where they or their cultures fit, where they are included, answering "So What?" and "Why do I care?" becomes more difficult. For our purposes, cultural relevance means students understand, first, where they fit in the historical record; and, second, why what they are learning is relevant to them. Cultural relevance implies that student backgrounds and culture are included in what they learn.

Cultural relevance is important because teaching and learning history has not always been inclusive. Not all peoples and cultures have had equal or any access to the history curriculum. Omissions, distortions, and biases affect the legitimacy of what students learn. Too often, what students learn is only half the story.

Changing the Half-Told Story

The seemingly infinite amount of historical content has always clashed with the finite reality of the time and space devoted to history education. How do teachers provide a coherent, cohesive story that promotes student learning? Or, more simply put, teachers can't teach everything so what determines what students learn?

Expanding the curriculum to be more representative is an ongoing challenge since the space and time constraints of courses and class sessions do not change. In addition, history education must meet the needs of an increasingly diverse student population. If students do not see people like themselves or if they only see negative content, they might question their relationship to society affecting their development as citizens. And they are certainly less motivated to learn.

As a result, race, ethnicity, and gender are major topics of reform, spurring the movement for cultural relevance and inclusion. Over time, the original idea of cultural relevance has expanded to include cultural responsiveness and culturally sustaining pedagogy.

Cultural Relevance, Cultural Responsiveness, and Culturally Sustaining

The current cultural relevance movement emerged in 1995 when educator Gloria Ladson-Billings defined culturally relevant pedagogy as a model of teaching that "not only addresses student achievement but also helps students to accept and affirm their cultural identity while developing critical perspectives that challenge inequities that schools (and other institutions) perpetuate."[7]

Over time, attention turned to related aspects of culture and identity. Geneva Gay focused on what teachers do, coining the term culturally responsive. She suggested teachers needed to use "the cultural knowledge, prior experiences, frames of reference, and performance styles of ethnically diverse students to make learning encounters more relevant to and effective for them."[8] Django Paris extended both ideas, stressing culturally sustaining, meaning teachers help students develop a positive cultural identity that sustains their culture.[9]

The expansive nature of culture relevance, responsiveness, sustainability, and inclusion is beyond the scope of this book. The focus here is on looking at what is being taught in history classes, so students see where they and their culture fit in the historical record. A first step is examining cultural relevance in state history curricula.

State Curricula and Cultural Relevance

Despite the history wars controversy over exceptionalism versus diversity, a 2019 New America survey concluded that all 50 states include culturally relevant teaching in their standards. So do the Council of Chief State School Officers' (CCSSO) Interstate Teacher Assessment and Support Consortium (InTASC) and National Board for Professional Teaching Standards (NBPTS). The distinction is in the specific requirements. Twenty-eight states ask teachers to reflect on their own cultural perspectives and biases, but only three states explicitly state that teachers should know about institutional biases.[10]

Each state provides a statement on cultural relevance in their standards. Illinois has a comprehensive description that includes anti-racism, recognizing any implicit bias, and using anti-bias approaches. Other states offer brief statements. Mississippi just asks teachers to be culturally responsive. Alaska's statement combines cultural relevance with inclusion, explaining that school districts should share "culturally relevant instructional practices and resources, especially in meeting the needs of minority students who are also English learners."[11]

One concern is the content being taught and from what perspective. Including cultural relevance is one thing but how the story is told is another. A major issue is the debate over the master narrative versus the diverse master narratives (diverse narratives) discussed in the introduction. Diverse narratives attempt to achieve cultural relevance by including all peoples and cultures in the teaching and learning of history. While more is involved, an important foundation of cultural relevance is inclusion.

Inclusion

In this context, inclusion means that all relevant peoples are represented when studying a topic or theme. Where pertinent, inclusion implies that the students' culture and people from their backgrounds are studied. Just noting who was included is not enough, nor is treating people or cultures as an added paragraph, a footnote, or a totally separate and distinct experience. The level of participation and contribution is also important. True inclusion involves integration, so students study a topic from several pertinent perspectives.

Integration for inclusion is quite a balancing act given the time and space constraints of history education. Inquiry-based learning eases the situation because by design it emphasizes diverse viewpoints. Primary sources often contain different perspectives. Critical literacy builds skills to closely examine documents for, on one hand, bias, omission, and distortion; and, on the other hand, for resistance, protest, and opposing opinions to the dominant culture.

An important aspect of history that may be neglected is the human side of the story told by those affected by historical events. While first-hand experiences and memories provide new content and insight, time and space considerations make integrating individual stories difficult. Yet, the individual stories enhance the culturally relevant and inclusive quality of history teaching and learning.

Numerous oral history projects and the growing online archives of primary sources provide abundant accounts by individuals on their personal experiences. By designing a DBQ (document-based question) examining first-hand experience as an activity theme, teachers bring history to life for students as the example below shows. An important caveat is that relevance and inclusion should extend beyond a single DBQ activity. What is presented here is just one idea.

Japanese Americans in World War II: A Diverse Master Narrative

Especially in recent years, history textbooks and courses have improved their telling of the Japanese American experience in World War II. The narrative focuses on two experiences: internment, or, as many Japanese Americans have called it, incarceration; and military service. In some cases, repatriation to Japan after the war and the successful Japanese American campaign for redress and reparations is briefly described. Regarding numbers, about 120,000 Japanese Americans were relocated to camps.[12]

Often missing from the narrative of Japanese Americans in World War II is the perspective of those who lived through these times. The one-day DBQ activity below provides students with first-hand accounts of the emotions and experiences of Japanese Americans who went to the camps and fought in the military. It is applicable for middle and high school.

While other questions are possible, for this example, the question is this: "How did Japanese Americans respond to how the United States treated them in World War II?" To answer the question, students read the following documents. Since World War II is studied later in the school year, no guiding questions for the reading are provided.

Incarceration

John Wakamatsu retold the story his father told him of his grandparents' removal to the Manzanar, California, camp. At the time, his father was in the U.S. Army and helped his parents relocate. The camp administrator asked if his father wanted to stay with his family for a while and he did. Recalling what his father told him, John Wakamtatsu said,

> Well, of course you've got to stay with your family. But, . . . walking around Manzanar with a U.S. Army uniform on is a rather strange experience 'cause he could leave, but his parents couldn't leave. So, . . . his parents were considered a risk, and yet he's in the military. So, . . . it doesn't make any sense to my dad.
>
> But he told me that he trained some of the soldiers that were guarding Manzanar at Fort Ord, so he told them that if they could be nice to his parents and his family. So, . . . you can imagine how they felt. My dad said as he left Manzanar he turned around and he said, . . . "This is not good." And then he drove back to Los Angeles, and he said it was a pretty lousy experience.[13]

Mary Suzuki Ichino was a teenager when her family was sent to Manzanar. She later wrote a letter to General DeWitt, commander of the Western Defense Command in charge of the interment program. Many years after the war, Ms. Ichino commented on her reaction to being relocated:

I thought, it's sort of like an adventure, you know, for a teenager, when you think about it. You're moving, you're going, you know. But when I started seeing that my dad is losing his business, we're losing all our property, he lost his new car that he worked so darn hard for—What for? We're not from Japan. You know? Then when finally we went to camp is when I realized the injustice of the whole thing. And you're always taught in civics in high school that we're all equal under the law, and I said, "But how can you be equal when you haven't had a hearing as to whether you're guilty or not guilty?"[14]

In the camps, the Japanese Americans built strong communities, including publishing a camp newspaper. The Tule Lake, California, newspaper was called the *Tulean Dispatch*. On March 27, 1943, as Figure 4.1 below shows, the paper published a poem by Sara Muryama called "Loyalty."[15] The picture of the guard tower that accompanied the poem offered a wry commentary on the experience.

Some Japanese Americans rebelled against incarceration. They angrily and sometimes violently reacted to their situation. Some wanted to return to Japan. Between 1943 and 1946, over 20,000 Japanese Americans applied to return to Japan with 4,724 going to Japan, though many later returned to the United States.[16]

Katsuma Mukaeda described one protest at a Louisiana camp:

Then the trouble began! Some of the rough, hardheaded boys, who gave up their American citizenship and wanted to go back to Japan, had something drawn on their shirt with the rising sun right on the front. That kind of thing is against the camp rules. The administration told them to take them off, but they didn't do it. They clashed with the officers of the camp after they were ordered to disband a meeting. The officers threw tear gas and then they disbanded. Before they did disband, some of the internees went along and spoke against the officers with dirty words. They got beaten up.[17]

Military Service

Approximately 33,000 Japanese Americans served in the military. Roy Matsumoto enlisted in the army after being sent to an incarceration camp. He served as a member of Merrill's Marauders Rangers in Burma. In February 1944, his company was surrounded by Japanese troops. Matsumoto infiltrated the Japanese camp and overheard their plans for attack. Returning to the U.S. camp, he told the commanding officer of the Japanese plans. The U.S. forces moved up a hill and boobytrapped empty foxholes. Matsumoto described what happened when the Japanese soldiers attacked:

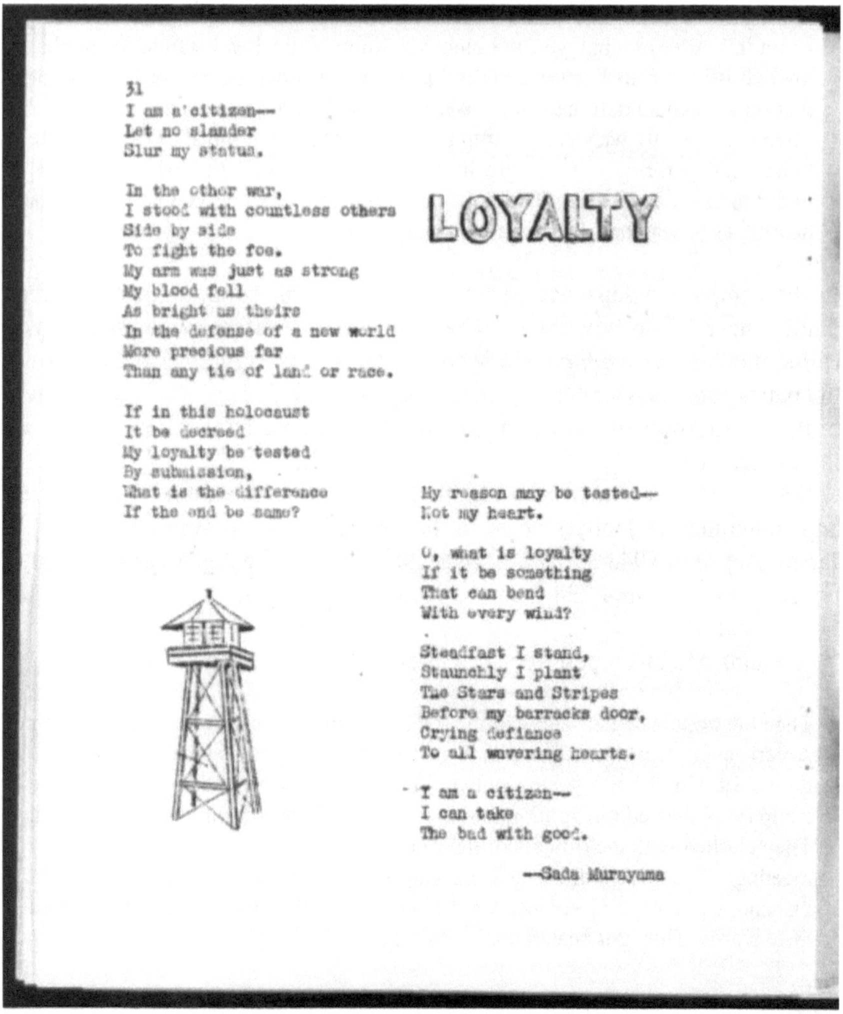

> 31
>
> I am a citizen—
> Let no slander
> Slur my status.
>
> **LOYALTY**
>
> In the other war,
> I stood with countless others
> Side by side
> To fight the foe.
> My arm was just as strong
> My blood fell
> As bright as theirs
> In the defense of a new world
> More precious far
> Than any tie of land or race.
>
> If in this holocaust
> It be decreed
> My loyalty be tested
> By submission,
> What is the difference
> If the end be same?
>
> My reason may be tested—
> Not my heart.
>
> O, what is loyalty
> If it be something
> That can bend
> With every wind?
>
> Steadfast I stand,
> Staunchly I plant
> The Stars and Stripes
> Before my barracks door,
> Crying defiance
> To all wavering hearts.
>
> I am a citizen—
> I can take
> The bad with good.
>
> —Sada Murayama

Figure 4.1. "Loyalty" by Sara Muryama. Muryama, Sara, "Loyalty," *The Tulean Dispatch* (Newell, CA), May 27 1943. https://www.loc.gov/item/sn85040043/1943-05-27/ed-1/.

As expected, the enemy made an all-out assault up the hill at dawn. We held our fire until the enemy charged into the line of foxholes. We then opened with some fifty automatic weapons . . . as well as carbines and hand grenades. The second wave of the enemy troops hesitated in confusion. At that moment, I stood up and gave the order to attack in Japanese. The troops obeyed my order, and they were mowed down. And so we were able to break the siege, defeat an enemy superior in numbers, and survive until the 1st and 3rd Battalions joined us.[18]

Fred Shiosaki fought in France. In October, 1944, he was a member of 442nd Regimental Combat Team that rescued a lost battalion that had been surrounded by German troops. During the battle to rescue the 221 soldiers in the "Lost Battalion," almost 150 members of the 442nd were killed and 1,800 were wounded.

Shiosaki recalled the final assault that ended the battle:

[A]fter the fourth day, fifth day, we started to move and move and move. And . . . this terrible firefight is taking place. . . . [T]he path goes this way and then we curve up to, to hit, finally, the German strongpoint. And just, artillery coming in, and rifle fire, small arms fire, . . . and so we're moving, and the firefight is going on. And a shell hits the tree above me, and I get knocked down, and Jesus . . . I said, "God, I'm hit." And one of the guys comes over to me and says, "Are you," pulls the sweater up, and there's a big piece of shrapnel in my side, and . . . I'm not bleeding a hell of a lot, but I'm bleeding. And the medic patches it up, puts something on it, that's it, so we keep going.

But as we cleared . . . the ridge[,] . . . there's Colonel Purcell [commanding officer], . . . six-feet-six, standing there and waving us on: "Come on, you guys, let's go, let's go." And I'm sure that that finally just did it. Everybody just moved, and suddenly in combat, you know the battle is over when the firearms stop, and it just quit, it just, whump, and it was quiet. . . . [A]nd, "My God, it's done." I don't know, there was just hardly anybody left.[19]

The above documents are just a small sample of the many primary sources available on the Japanese American experience. They show the range of emotions and responses incarceration evoked in those affected. The incarceration documents highlight the irony and hypocrisy many Japanese Americans felt about the government actions. They also indicate that some rebelled against being incarcerated and wanted to return to Japan. The military experiences dramatically describe the horror of combat and the bravery of the Japanese American soldiers who served at the front.

Regarding the 442nd Battalion, it is the most decorated military unit in U.S. history. Members earned more than 18,000 awards, including 9,500 Purple Hearts. In addition, the Japanese American soldiers were awarded 5,200 Bronze Star Medals, 588 Silver Stars, 52 Distinguished Service Crosses, 7 Distinguished Unit Citations, and one Congressional Medal of Honor.

The DBQ in Perspective

After reading the documents and answering the question, students can better understand the real-life experience of the Japanese Americans in World War II. They learn another half of history's story. In addition, as the above example shows, one-day DBQ activities are a viable way for teachers to provide first-hand accounts of the experiences of diverse people in various events. When used in combination with other activities over time, such as the group presentations described in the preface. they seamlessly integrate diverse narratives into the flow of teaching and learning.

CONCLUSION

The title of this chapter, "Whose History?," raises an important question about what students should learn. Should students be able to "see" themselves in what they study? Yes. Effective history education increases student understanding of who they are and how and why the past affected their cultures, their ancestors, their families, and themselves. The old adage that history belongs to the victors has somewhat given way to the idea that history belongs to everyone. Relevance and inclusion have become watchwords of history education from the classroom to the state board of education to the U.S. Congress.

This chapter explored approaches that make history teaching and learning more relevant and inclusive. Using themes helps students see how and why the past connects to the present and to their lives. Approaching history from a diverse master narrative enables students to learn history that includes the different peoples and cultures of the world and the United States.

How does the concept of diverse master narratives influence teaching and learning? The following three chapters explore how the triad of inquiry, primary sources, and literacy offer teachers opportunities to ensure students learn as many of history's stories as possible. In the process, they build important skills that will serve them well in the subsequent education and life.

NOTES

1. Noah Kramer, "Schooldays: A Sumerian Composition Relating to the Education a Scribe," *Journal of the American Oriental Society* 69, no. 4 (October–December, 1949): 199–215.

2. Kramer, "Schooldays," 205.

3. CASEL, *CASEL'S SEL Framework* (Chicago, IL: Collaborative for Academic, Social, and Emotional Learning, 2020), 1.

4. Karen VanAusdel, "Collaborative Classrooms Support Social-Emotional Learning," *ASCD* 14, no. 22 (April 4, 2019): https://www.ascd.org/el/articles/collaborative-classrooms-support-social-emotional-learning.

5. Jean-Jacques Rousseau, *The Social Contract*. Trans. Charles Fankel (New York: Hefner Publishing Company, 1947), 14–15.

6. "The Constitution of the United States: A Transcription," America's Founding Documents, National Archives, https://www.archives.gov/founding-docs/constitution-transcript.

7. Gloria Ladson-Billings, "Toward a Theory of Culturally Relevant Pedagogy," *American Educational Research Journal* 32, no. 3 (Autumn 1995): 469.

8. Geneva Gay, *Culturally Responsive Teaching: Theory, Research, and Practice* (New York: Teachers College Press, 2010), 31.

9. Django Paris, "Culturally Sustaining Pedagogy: A Needed Change in Stance, Terminology, and Practice," *Educational Researcher* 41, no. 3 (March 2012): 95, https://doi.org/10.3102/0013189X12441244.

10. Jenny Muniz, *Culturally Responsive Teaching: A 50-State Survey of Teaching Standards* (Washington, DC: New America, 2019), 16, 17, 20, 21, https://newamerica.org/education-policy/reports/culturally-responsive-teaching/.

11. Isabella Schettino, Katherine Radvany, and Amy Stuart Wells, "Culturally Responsive Education Under ESSA: A State-By-State Snapshot," *Phi Delta Kappan* 101, no. 2 (September 23, 2019): 28–29.

12. Brian Niiya, "Ask a Historian: How Many Japanese Americans Were Incarcerated during WWII?" *Densho* (June 21, 2021): https://densho.org/catalyst/how-many-japanese-americans-were-incarcerated-during-wwii/.

13. John Wakamatsu, The Manzanar Oral History Project, n.d., https://www.nps.gov/museum/exhibits/manz/oral_history_videos.html.

14. Mary Ichino, The Manzanar Oral History Project, n.d., https://www.nps.gov/museum/exhibits/manz/oral_history_videos.html.

15. Sara Muryama, "Loyalty," *The Tulean Dispatch* (Newell, CA), May. 27 1943, https://www.loc.gov/item/sn85040043/1943-05-27/ed-1/.

16. Expatriation/repatriation/deportation, Densho Digital Repository (2023), https://ddr.densho.org/browse/topics/107/.

17. Katsuma Mukaeda, interview by Paul Clark, May 2, 1975, California State University, Fullerton Oral History Program Japanese American Project: http://texts.cdlib.org/view?docId=ft18700334&brand=calisphere&doc.view=entire_text.

18. Roy Matusmoto Oral History Interview, part 7 of 8, September 24, 2001, JAMHC: Japanese American Military History Collective, https://ndajams.omeka.net/items/show/432.

19. Fred Shiosaki, interview (2006), "Rescue of the Lost Battalion," Densho Encyclopedia, https://ddr.densho.org/media/ddr-densho-1000/ddr-densho-1000-190-transcript-fl46cb4c46.htm.

Chapter 5

World History

In a middle or high school world history course, an important question to answer is "Whose world are we studying?" During a time when cultural relevance is a foundational educational concept, the "whose world" question is more pressing, Students should understand that the world they envision is not necessarily everybody's world. Depending upon where they live, middle and high school students study very different pictures of the world in their history classes. To increase student understanding of the differing perspectives in world history, ask students to view two current world maps used in schools in the United States and East Asia.

In U.S. schools, the traditional world map is centered vertically on the Prime Meridian (0° longitude) that runs through Greenwich, England. Europe, Africa, and the eastern part of the Americas take center stage on this Atlantic-centered map while East Asia is at the edge. The world map shown in Figure 5.1 below is similar to maps commonly used in East Asian schools.[1] It is centered on the International Date Line (180° longitude) in the Pacific Ocean. East Asia, Australia, and the Pacific coast of the Americas occupy the middle. Europe, Africa, and the eastern portion of the Americas are relegated to the edges.

While the two maps depict different pictures of the world, they also have similarities that provide insight into the ways and means of world history. Both maps center the world around an ocean and an agreed upon longitudinal division of the planet. The Prime Meridian could be drawn anywhere on the globe. At one time, China set 0° longitude, so it ran through Beijing, France had it run through Paris, and so on.

In 1884, the International Meridian Conference, a convention of 21 nations met in Washington DC (26 had been invited). The participants included representatives from nations in North and South America, Europe, Africa, and Asia. They agreed to use the Greenwich Meridian as 0° longitude and 180° longitude as the International Date Line. Both maps use the same line, but they do so on opposite sides of the world.

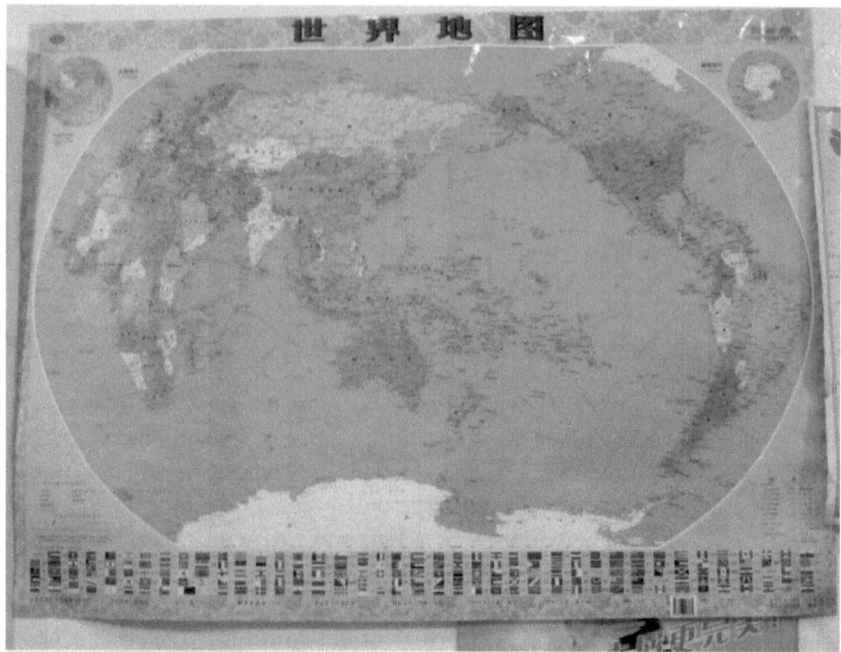

Figure 5.1. Chinese world map.

According to the Royal Museums Greenwich, there were two reasons why the Prime Meridian passes through Greenwich, England. First, the United States had already selected Greenwich as the basis for its national time zone system, highlighting a major reason for establishing it as the Prime Meridian. By the 1880s, organizing time on a global basis was important, in part due to the other reason for choosing Greenwich. In the late 1800s, almost 75% of world commerce depended upon maps using Greenwich as the Prime Meridian.[2]

The reasons behind choosing Greenwich as 0° longitude show the global influence of the United States, Europe, and maritime trade in the late nineteenth century. The United States set the precedent for using Greenwich in 1883, one year before the nation hosted the International Meridian Conference. Both actions highlight the growing global leadership of the United States The choice of the western standard for 0° longitude reflected the supremacy of the West and Great Britain during the age of imperialism, as did the dominance of the Greenwich Prime Meridian on maps. In the 1880s, the British Empire included territories on every continent except Antarctica.

As the above example shows, teaching world history provides teachers with opportunities to connect commonplace aspects of life to the global historical record. Classroom maps show the diversity and yet the unity of people and cultures. The choice of the Prime Meridian relates to a major factor of everyday life, time. In Chapter 4, we saw how a school day connected life in ancient civilizations to today.

CHAPTER OVERVIEW

This chapter explores the teaching and learning of world history. Three questions focus the discussion:

1. How can the history of the world be organized for teaching and learning in Grades 6–12?
2. How can periodization and themes help organize the massive, often disorderly historical record of the world into a cohesive, coherent, diverse, and relevant narrative?
3. How does the triad of inquiry-based learning, primary sources, and literacy make world history come alive for middle and high school students?

STUDYING THE HISTORY OF THE WORLD

Historians, teachers, and students face a similar dilemma. How do you organize the history of the world from beginning to end so that it encompasses the entire planet—and possibly beyond? Where does history start? What is included and what is left out? The questions animating debate over organizing the study of world history profoundly affect queries regarding its teaching and learning.

Since ancient times, philosophers, historians, geographers, at least one novelist, social scientists, and one ornithologist turned historian-geographer, among others, developed ideas on how to study the history of our world. The numerous attempts to examine world history over time and space have generated its own historiography, the story of its history.

The History of World History

The historiography of world history is too large and expansive to discuss here. What follows is a brief synopsis. The beginnings of human attempts to make sense of their world date back to antiquity. Oral traditions and religious texts explain the creation of the world. Often, they tell the history of a people, including interaction with other peoples and cultures. The discipline of history arose in two centers of classical culture: Greece and China. Herodotus, the father of history in the West, chronicled the Greek-Persian wars and wrote about other peoples. The fathers of history in the East, Sima Quan and Ban Gu, wrote histories of the Han dynasty.[3]

Several later developments deserve mention. In the 14th century, Muslim scholar Ibn Khaldun developed principles regarding the interaction between states and societies. European Enlightenment philosophers Voltaire, Montesquieu, and Leibniz advanced the field with their comparative studies of societies. In the 19th century, German philosopher G. W. F. Hegel developed the dialectic of thesis, antithesis, and synthesis to explain how societies developed. Karl Marx adapted the dialectic to explain his ideas on historical materialism.

During the 20th and 21st centuries, the academic field of world history blossomed, becoming a valuable component of the larger discipline of history. The so-called philosophers of history school emerged after World War I. Among others, Oswald Spengler, Arnold Toynbee, novelist H. G. Wells, and Karl Jaspers emphasized the study of large-scale, complex societies they called civilizations. They also noted the importance of cross-cultural interactions.

In the post–World War II era, social scientists studied modernization and dependency. They also pioneered the concept of world-system analysis. Regarding modernization, Cyril E. Black suggested that in becoming modern, traditional societies experienced a series of transformations: intellectual, political, economic, and social. Later studies focused on comparative analysis in various nations.

In the 1960s, Andre Gunder Frank used dependency theory to explain modern world history. Colonialism and imperialism underscored modern world development, establishing the hegemony of Western capitalist nations and the underdevelopment of the Third World. The concepts of metropolis (imperial and colonial powers) and satellites (imperial and colonial cities and centers in subject lands) explained how wealth was extracted from the subject lands. The extraction of wealth fueled the development of metropolitan nations while blocking similar development in the exploited lands.

Dependency theory influenced the rise of world-system analysis by Emmanuel Wallerstein and others. Wallerstein expanded Frank's concept of metropolis and satellite into three categories. Core and periphery are similar to metropolis and satellite. Semiperiphery refers to lands whose economy moved up or down in the world-system. In addition, Wallerstein focused on long-term, large-scale economic cycles that determined the movement of the entire world-system. Historians have applied world-system analysis to the modern, premodern, and the ancient world. One issue is that the Western-centric bias of dependency theory and world-system analysis heightens the impact of the West downplaying non-Western interests and ideas.

In the last several decades, another trend has been to move away from a Eurocentric view of world history to a more equitable global context. In the 1950s, Marshall G. S. Hodgson argued for a hemispheric interregional approach to world history that abandoned what he considered a "Westward distortion."[4] Recent works have also rejected a Western perspective. Robert B. Marks stresses the roles China and India played in his *The Origins of the Modern World*. In *The Silk Road, A New History of the World*. Peter Frankopan emphasizes the role played by the Eurasian steppe and Persia (present-day Iran) in the history of the world.[5]

Other works emphasized cross-cultural diffusion. William H. McNeill's *The Rise of the West* suggested that because they introduce something new into a society, contacts between different peoples and cultures are a major agent of change in human history. McNeill applied that idea to a global context in books on disease and power as well as his world history textbook, *A History of the Human Community: Prehistory to the Present* (1987).[6] Lynda Shaffer examined the influence of South and Southeast Asia on other areas of the world in her article on Southernization. Technological diffusion has been the subject of several books.[7]

Large-scale histories also have increased understanding of the world. K. N. Chaudhuri examined how trade led to economic integration in the Indian Ocean basin prior to modern times. In his studies of the African slave trade and plantations, Philip Curtin suggested that political, social, and economic influences among peoples from four continents created an integrated Atlantic world. He expanded his analysis in *Cross Cultural Trade in World History*. An intriguing approach is David Christian's idea of big history that connects the history of the earth to that of the universe.[8]

The final school to be discussed here is large-scale environmental and ecological history. These works analyze the impact of environmental, ecological, and biological processes generally on trans-regional, transcontinental, and global scales. Alfred Crosby evaluated the impact of the Columbian Exchange. He also looked at why certain European animals, plants, and people spread in some parts of the world, but not others. Jared Diamond examined how environmental and technological factors influenced the development of world societies. Joachim Radkau's *Nature and Power* is a global environmental history.[9]

The various schools of thought are one component of the attempt to make sense of the world. Both for study and, more importantly, for teaching, another effort seeks to provide a workable chronology. Periodization, as it is known, also has generated much discussion.

World History Periodization

The most obvious issue involved in organizing world history by era is creating a periodization that works on a global scale. Outside of a brief foray by the Norse in Canada, the lack of contact between the eastern and western hemispheres meant cultures developed differently at different times before 1492. How to accommodate the variations has been a major concern. In one way or another, the same discrepancy applies to every other part of the world. The late 1980s and 1990s witnessed a renewed concern regarding periodizing world history for study and teaching.

Periodization organizes world history chronologically into eras. The traditional Western Civilization model was ancient, medieval, and modern. Historian William A. Green called the three-category model a "straitjacket," adding the newness of world history allowed it to escape the tripartite model's "insidious" influence.[10] Green advised that the objectives in teaching world history influence its periodization.

Green identified two approaches to organizing world history. The integrationist concept offers an "unintegrated mainstream treatment of world history."[11] This model concentrates on the life cycles of the most developed, complex societies, emphasizing Eurasia, but neglecting Sub-Saharan Africa, pre-Columbian America, and Australia and Oceania for long periods of time. The regional approach stresses regional diversity. It accommodates more of the world's peoples and cultures over time, focusing on intercultural understanding. But that same diversity and inclusiveness inhibits the posing of large theories of change applicable to the entire world.

No matter what approach is adopted, the issue remains on how to chart out world history into viable eras for teaching and learning. Historians, commissions, and textbook publishers have devised numerous periodization models. Some divide world history into large-scale eras spanning millennia. Others favor more eras over shorter periods of time. Recognizing that ideas can change, Table 5.1 shows the variety of available models.[12]

The examples in Table 5.1 follow a progression in which the time frame of the eras decrease as the present day is approached. Christian, McNeill, and Stearns chart a course over time that culminates with the idea of a single world community. McNeill, Stearns, Bentley, and the UCLA National Standards provide a brief description of each era. The UCLA model is not just a periodization. It also provides standards for world history.

The question of periodization remains a topic of discussion, especially regarding updating eras to accommodate the 21st century. Another concern is how well any periodization fits within a school curriculum. Often, the textbook provides the organization but, in many schools, teachers do not use textbooks, opting for developing their own course organization by compiling

Table 5.1. History Periodization Models

David Christian	William McNeill	Peter Stearns	Jerry Bentley	UCLA National Standards
Many Worlds: Paleolithic and Beginnings of Human History, 300,000/250,000–10,000–500BP	Beginnings to 500 3CE	Development of Agriculture and Emergence of Civilization, 9,000–3,500BCE	Age of Early Complex Societies, 3,500–2,500BCE	Beginnings of Human Society, to 4,000BCE
Few Worlds: Holocene and Agrarian Era, 10,000–500BP	Classical World and Its Expansion, 500BCE–1,500 CE	Expansion of Civilization to Wider Human Interaction, 3,500–500BCE	Age of Ancient Civilizations, 2,000–500BCE	Early Civilizations and Emergence of Pastoral Peoples, 4,000–1,000BCE
One World: 500BP–Prsent	Far West Challenges the World 1500–1850CE	First Era of Inter-Civilization Contacts, 500BCE–500CE	Age of Classical Civilizations, 500BCE–500CE	Classical Traditions, Major Religions, Great Empires, 1,000BCE–300CE
	Beginnings of World Cosmopolitanism, 1850–Present	Emergence of New Civilizations, Expanded Commercial Relations, Monotheistic Religion Dominance, 500–1,500CE	Post Classical Age, 500–1,000CE	Expanding Zones of Exchange and Encounter, 300–1,000 CE
		Complex World Economy, Industrialization, Western Domination, 1,500CE–Present	Age of Transregional Nomadic Empires, 1,000–1,500 CE	Intensified Hemispheric Interactions, 1,000–1,500 CE
			Modern Age 1,500 CE–Present	Emergence of the First Global Age, 1450–1770
				Age of Revolutions, 1750–1914 CE
				Half-Century of Crisis and Achievement, 1900–1945
				20th Century Since 1945: Promises and Paradoxes

a set of readings and other materials. Often teachers use themes to organize their courses.

Themes as Organizers

In addition to organizing the world by eras, some models include major themes that cut across the periods. By studying themes across units, students become more familiar with the terms and increase their competency in applying them in their studies.

Stearns, McNeill, and Bentley identify themes that span their respective eras. Stearns identifies three themes:

1. Basic technology shifts
2. Changes in patterns of commercial exchange
3. Development of belief systems[13]

Both McNeill and Bentley emphasize cross-cultural interaction as a major theme in world history. Drawing upon the work of anthropologists, McNeill stresses cultural diffusion, claiming the meeting of different cultures became "the driving wheel of history." Bentley suggested that a focus on cross-cultural interactions would help identify patterns of continuity and change among many cultures.[14]

How well do those themes work in the Grades 6–12 world history classroom? Both Stearns and McNeill wrote popular world history textbooks that went through several editions. But, as noted above, many teachers do not use textbooks, preferring to develop their own readings and materials. In some cases, teachers adapt the core social studies subjects of civics (political science), economics, geography, and social sciences as themes for a world history course.

Each of the social studies subject areas can be broken down into sub-themes that are more specific and descriptive. A partial list of possibilities includes the following:

- *political systems*: sovereignty, government, constitutionalism, rule of law, human rights
- *economic systems*: use of scarce resources, redistributive, exchange, market, self-sufficiency
- *geography*: location, place, regions, movement, human-environmental interaction
- *social-cultural systems*: race, class, gender, belief and thought, societal organization, the arts, and literature

In addition, themes can encompass more than one subject area. Some examples include war and peace, technology, and everyday life.

When the world history course focuses on cultures or civilizations, the life cycle of a civilization is a likely overarching theme. Anthropologist Anthony F. C. Wallace's revitalization theory offers a way to plot the life cycle of a culture or civilization. Wallace defines revitalization as "a deliberate, organized, conscious effort by members of a society to construct a more satisfying culture."[15] It is a unique type of cultural change that overtly seeks to replace unsatisfactory cultural elements with new ones. The end result is often a new cultural system.

The life cycle begins when local cultures arise leading to the emergence of a dominant group. Development continues to a high point, perhaps a golden age or empire, followed by a period of decline that ends in disappearance or revitalization. Not all revitalization efforts succeed, nor do they necessarily return the culture to its former glory. Wallace cites numerous examples of cultural revitalization movements, including the origins of Christianity and Islam, the early development of Sikkhism in India (ca.1500–1700). Other examples include the Xosa Revival in South Africa in 1856–1857, and the Sudan Mahdi rebellion between 1880 and 1898.

The life cycle approach provides a linear way to study a culture or civilization. As is true of all the examples discussed here, it attempts to make sense of the complex history of the world. It also provides a structure for Grades 6–12 history teachers to design an effective world history course.

The remainder of the chapter explores ways of using this combination of ideas in the classroom from designing a course to developing activities.

DESIGNING A WORLD HISTORY COURSE

In designing a world history course, two questions are important:

1. How is the course being taught to maximize student learning?
2. How is the content being organized?

In this book, the first question is easily answered. Students actively engage the triad, conducting inquiry to analyze primary and other sources by practicing literacy skills. As discussed in Chapter 1, the inquiry process structures teaching and learning. The compelling question drives learning. Students begin with a big picture overview followed by in-depth case studies. The process concludes with the summative assessment. Students synthesize and make meaning of what they learned to answer the compelling question.

The second question on organizing content requires careful thought. Three content-based approaches are available: chronological, thematic, and a hybrid of the two. Each method has its strengths and weaknesses.

The chronological approach follows a timeline of units that go from past to present. Advocates suggest that students cannot understand history unless they develop the chronological reasoning skills embedded in the chronological approach. They claim the chronological is the most effective model because it is appropriate for all ages. Teachers also report that it is a familiar method that is easy to understand and helps students comprehend cause and effect relationships. Some teachers use an innovative chronological approach moving back from the present to the past.

Critics argue that the chronological approach is boring to students because it promotes memorization, the old complaint that history is just names and dates. Because it often employs a survey model, critics also claim the chronological approach tries to teach everything so it does not lead to full learning or teach skills.[16] The issue may be the survey method rather than the chronological approach.

The thematic method stresses central themes but does not necessarily abandon chronology. Supporters say the thematic approach helps students develop inquiry skills, making history more meaningful and appealing to students. They also claim using a specific theme to study a series of events helps students better understand cause and effect relationships. Other advantages include promoting use of student-centered methods and teaching multiple perspectives.

Critics say the thematic approach is difficult to implement and is hard for students to understand, it is not suitable for all ages. They also say the thematic approach can be repetitive.[17] Here, too, method is important. Inquiry organizes themes into a comprehensible context that facilitates learning.

The hybrid approach combines the chronological and the thematic. Supporters explain that the hybrid combines the advantages of both approaches while limiting their disadvantages. Here are some examples:

- chronological approach but identifying a central theme for a week, unit, era, or century
- chronological but stressing group work on themes
- thematic but arranging them in chronological order
- thematic but integrating chronology[18]

A hybrid chronological-thematic approach promotes progressive learning that builds student content understanding and skills mastery. The basic structure is chronological. The unit topics move from past to present in representative rather than attempted comprehensive fashion. The chronology includes the broad eras noted above by the various historians. Within each era, unit topics exemplify aspects of that time period or span several examples under a larger construct that facilitates a combination of big picture and in-depth study. For example, early civilizations may focus exclusively on river valley civilizations.

Themes organize the content so students study similar concepts in each unit, promoting progressive learning over time. As students become familiar with content concepts, vocabulary, and as they work with thematic concepts multiple times, they build on past learning. Initially, students need to learn what the concepts are and how they work. They need to define general vocabulary terms. After they understand the concepts and know the meaning of the terms, students apply them to new learning at higher levels of complexity increasing content knowledge and skills proficiency.

The Influence of Local Conditions

In all history courses and other subjects, local conditions exert a strong influence on course design. Basically, what is required and what is most effective for student learning largely determines the course design. The school district or school may have an approved curriculum based on state standards that teachers must follow. In 46 states, inquiry is the mandated method. Teacher content knowledge of world history is another determinant as is student prior knowledge of the world and approaches to learning. Student demographics is a consideration. Teachers can include study of student cultural backgrounds to increase relevance.

Part of the design process includes answering some basic questions that may or may not be mandated by the powers that be:

1. Will students study cultures and civilizations?
2. Will a regional or global perspective be used?
3. Or will there be a combination of both?

Determining factors are the scope and scale of the content to be studied and the time allotted for learning, the length of the unit. The example below is a large regional (or global) unit that encompasses several civilizations during a specific time period. The description assumes all of the culture/civilizations will be studied over eight or more weeks. But, if time is an issue, examples could be reduced or the unit can be divided into two units.

The Axial Age

German philosopher Karl Jasper's axial age of civilization concept organizes the history of the Eurasian world spatially during a specific time period.[19] Between approximately 800 and 200 BCE, Jaspers suggested was an axial age in the Mediterranean, Middle East, India, and China that established the foundations of thought and religion for the modern world. Greek, Indian, and Chinese philosophy developed. Greek drama emerged. Hebrews created the prophetic tradition that underscores Judaism, Christianity, and Islam. In Persia, Zoroaster taught about the struggle between good and evil. In India, the Upanishads were written and Buddha lived.

Building on the axial age concept, world history teachers have two options. They can design a hybrid approach, classical age unit. Replacing axial with classical, but keeping Jasper's definition, provides students with a more familiar term used in textbooks and other resources. By expanding the time frame to 800 BCE–400 CE, study expands to include the Roman, Han, and Mauryan empires; the rise of Christianity; and later developments in Hinduism and Buddhism. Though other options exist, students study each civilization individually and then comparatively using the following themes: philosophy, religion, government, and technology.

As shown in the weekly schedule below, this unit would be nine weeks long:

- *Week 1*: introduction to classical age concept, overview maps of civilizations, big picture timeline, and orientation to themes
- *Weeks 2–8*: one- or two-week study each of Greece, Rome, India, and China, including first week overview and second week case study. If time does not permit, then each civilization would have one week, with one or two days devoted to the case study
- *Week 9*: synthesis of learning, summative assessment, and conclusion

An important aspect is making sure students understand what a classical age is. A solution is to have the compelling question be this: "What characterizes a classical age?" For each civilization the supporting question is "What characterized (insert civilization) as a classical age?"

Students study each culture/civilization in the same way. They complete maps and timelines of each civilization. They also complete a table using the characteristics: philosophy, religion, government, and technology. Next, they conduct an in-depth study of an important aspect or aspects of the culture/civilization relevant to a foundation of modern society. To close the study of the civilization, students synthesize and make meaning of what they learned to answer the supporting question. Because the content changes, the civilization studies do not become repetitive. Instead, students practice tasks over time to improve their skills and knowledge.

The final task is synthesizing what was learned about the various civilizations. Students create a hemispheric map of the cultures/civilizations and a multicultural/civilizations timeline. A Venn diagram allows them to compare and contrast the cultures/civilizations and also compare the findings of the in-depth studies. To end the unit, students answer the compelling question, perhaps using the findings of the Venn diagram.

A different option divides the above unit into two. The first unit focuses on the axial age as defined by Jaspers and would stress religion and philosophy. The following unit would continue the study by examining the classical empires. The two-unit study offers an ability to expand the content of the classical age concept to the Maya in Mesoamerica and Axum in Africa, providing a global perspective.

Depending upon time, the axial/classical age concept is easily adapted to other topics. Early civilizations are a prime example. By loosening the time frame, students study early civilizations in Egypt/Nubia, Mesopotamia, the Indus River Valley, China, and possibly the Olmec in Mesoamerica.

The industrial revolution and imperialism/decolonization can also be studied with this approach. The industrial revolution and imperialism/decolonization span a large time frame. Starting with Great Britain, the industrial revolution occurred at various times in different nations including the United States, Japan, Germany, Russia, and China, among others. The same is true of imperialism/decolonization. Both topics raise important issues regarding use of resources, wealth accumulation and disparity, and, as explained below, child labor.

Connecting Past and Present: Child Labor

The axial age/classical concept is not the only approach to world history. Some themes connect students to the everyday lives of past contemporaries enhancing the relevance of what is studied. Assume that a course theme is everyday life with special attention to the lives of children. The activity on Mesopotamian schools that opened Chapter 4 is an example. In a later unit on the Industrial Revolution, child labor is a likely topic that also connects to the present.

In two ways, child labor has special relevance for students, especially those working outside the home. First, throughout history, children have been part of the workforce, often laboring in family agriculture or herding. During the Industrial Revolution, child labor expanded to other work sectors, stimulating reform efforts that exposed the dire conditions under which many young children worked. Second, in nations around the world, including the United States, many children labor under similar conditions today.[20]

Inquiry-based learning opens opportunities for students to participate in activities that bring them closer to the people, places, and times being studied. Many examples exist such as trials and role plays. For example, regarding child labor, in a role-play simulation, students assume personas of child workers, so they walk in their shoes, so to speak. The activities also can be extended to explore child labor in the world and the United States today among their contemporaries.

Child Labor Over Time and Place

Child labor provides an excellent opportunity for students to connect past and present, often to their own working conditions. The discussion examines child labor in Great Britain in the mid-1800s and moves to child labor today in the world and the United States.

Child Labor in Great Britain

Child labor was a major topic of concern in Great Britain in the 19th century. Children worked in virtually every industry in the United Kingdom, but much attention has been paid to textile factories and mines. Several government investigations and various studies showed the number of children working in these industries and described their working conditions. For the simulation, ask students to assume the identity of English child laborers and possibly bosses in textile factories and coal mines. Depending upon the type of simulation, students might also portray investigators looking at child labor.

A large number of resources on child labor in England in the mid-1800s are easily accessed. The relevant primary sources tend to fall into three general categories: statistics, visuals of children working, and testimony of child laborers before government commissions. Often the pictures and interviews can be found in books published as exposés of child labor or commission reports.

Statistics provide a big-picture overview of child labor in England. The focus here is on mines and textile factories. Charles Booth's 1886 study of industry, work, and population in England and Wales, Scotland, and Ireland reported that in 1851:

- 32,400 males under 15; 42,600 males between 15 and 20; and 1,400 females under 15 worked in the mines; and
- 68,000 males under 15; 75,800 males between 15 and 20; and 81,300 females under 15 worked in a textile factory.[21]

Exposés generally contained pictures and excerpts of interviews with child laborers. The visuals and interviews provide present-day students with graphic and dramatic descriptions of child labor working conditions. A teacher might comment that some of the children testifying were younger than the students in class.

In 1853, John C. Cobden published *The White Slaves of England* that included sections on child labor. The title page picture below (Figure 5.2) shows a young boy holding up his hands for protection as he is beaten with a strap in a textile factory.[22] Children were strapped for such offenses as talking to another child or falling asleep at work.

Physical punishment was prevalent in the factories. In *The White Slaves of England*, Thomas Clarke, age 11, reported the following:

> Badder [his former employer] used to strap me some odd times. Some odd times he'd catch me over the head, but it was mostly on the back. He made me sing out. . . . He would strap us about twelve times at once. He used to strap us sometimes over the head.[23]

Children also worked in coal mines, performing various tasks, often in tight places. Figure 5.3 below shows children hurrying (pulling) and thrusting (pushing) a loaded corve (mine cart) that could weigh several hundred pounds through passages between 16 and 20 inches in height.[24] They crawled on their hands and feet for an average of 150 yards and made about 16 trips both ways. On one trip, the corve was fully loaded. It was empty on the return trip.

Testifying before the Children's Employment Commission in the early 1840s, Harriet Morton, age 14, explained how hurrying and thrusting worked:

> Two of us are employed at each corve both full and empty. When the corve is loaded, one of us is harnessed with a belt round the waist, and a chain comes from the front of the belt and passes betwixt our legs and is hooked on to the corve, and we go along on our hands and feet, on all—fours. I do so myself, and a little boy pushes behind.[25]

Child Labor in the World Today

Statistics show that child labor today is a global phenomenon. In 2021, *Child Labour: Global Estimates 2020, Trends and the Road Forward* reported the following:

- 160 million children worldwide were working in some capacity, representing an increase of 8.4 million children over the last four years
- Over 50% of working children are between 5 and 11 years old

FIFTH THOUSAND.

THE WHITE SLAVES

OF

ENGLAND.

COMPILED FROM OFFICIAL DOCUMENTS.

WITH TWELVE SPIRITED ILLUSTRATIONS.

BY JOHN C. COBDEN.

Figure 5.2. *The White Slaves of England* by John C. Cobden. Cobden, John C., *The White Slaves of England*, Miller Orton and Mulligan (Auburn, England and Buffalo, New York) 1854, title page. Project Gutenberg. https://www.gutenberg.org/files/52423/52423-h/52423-h.htm.

GIRL WITH COAL CART IN THIN SEAM;

Figure 5.3. Children working in a coal mine.

- The number of children between 5 and 17 working in hazardous conditions, meaning the job is likely to harm their health, has risen from 72.5 million in 2016 to 79 million in 2021
- Agriculture employs 70% of children (112 million), services 20% (31.4 million), and industry (16.5 million).[26]

In addition to the above statistics, the report explained why children work, noting the impact of the COVID-19 pandemic:

> Most children who work do so because their families depend on their wages, production or domestic work (including unpaid, often by girls) to make ends meet. Household economic shocks and the loss of a parent or caregiver can increase the chance that a child will go to work. Even before the COVID-19 pandemic, nearly one in three children in low- and middle-income countries lived in families below national poverty lines. The pandemic exacerbated child poverty, with the number of children in income-poor households increasing by over 142 million in 2020.[27]

In the United States, a recent and growing phenomenon is the labor of underage migrant children, many of whom come from Central America to the United States without family members. The *New York Times* called the employment of unaccompanied migrant children a "shadow work force that extends across industries in every state, flouting child labor laws that have been in place of nearly a century."[28] The *Times* noted that the children enter the country legally. Many work at night and then go to school during the day. Some only work. Many children work long hours in hazardous conditions in meatpacking plants, slaughterhouses, on farms, and in food processing companies, among others.

As the above discussion shows, just as it did in the 19th century, child labor remains an integral and troublesome part of the world economy. Many young people have part-time jobs that allow them to earn money in favorable situations, while many others work part or full time under harsh, often dangerous conditions. The wealth of resources available on child labor combined with its strong connection to student everyday lives make it an excellent topic of study in middle and high school history classes.

Classroom Activities

Child labor can be explored through a variety of activities. A key is having students assume the identities of child laborers—they "step into their shoes" to experience history. Groups of students could write and perform dramatic scenes of children working. They might create videos or infographics on child labor.

As noted above, role play simulations are another option. Depending upon the simulation, they can make decisions to engage in civic action regarding child labor today. If student employment experiences are used, most likely in high school, the starting point is surveying the students to see if any of them have a current job or if they have worked in the past. Ask them to write a short description of the job including the hours and days worked, the tasks performed, their tenure at the job, and how their employers treated them. These students portray themselves in the simulation.

The example here has students draw upon their own employment experience where relevant, to examine child labor in England in the mid-1800s, and to explore it around the world today. Students assume the identities of child workers testifying before a commission (composed of students) investigating child labor. As a summative assignment, ask the students to use the findings of the commission to develop a bill of rights for child labor.

Technology in Global Perspective

Technological invention and innovation is an important theme in world history and often has been a multicultural affair. Almost every major culture developed a strong technological sector that influenced its development. In some cases, the development was internal while, in other instances, technology was borrowed from another culture and further developed.

For example, during the transoceanic encounter of the 15th and 16th centuries, multicultural influences contributed to the design of European ships and navigation aids. The compass, flat stern, gunpowder, and cannons originally came from China. Islamic cultures contributed cannon design, multiple masts and sail design, and probably the astrolabe for determining latitude.[29]

Classroom Activities

A variety of activities can help students inquire into the technological contributions made by different cultures. Students can construct a multicultural pictorial timeline of inventions that includes a visual of the invention or perhaps links to a video that shows how the invention works. They can collaborate with a science class to build an invention.

Games are another possibility. Games are valuable classroom activities that can be used as hooks to assess prior knowledge and to open a unit. Many teachers use games for review before an assessment. Numerous game options exist. One popular technology-based game is Kahoot that engages students in a friendly competition. Students are given a time frame to answer questions and then the game shows how many chose the correct answer. Scores are tabulated after each round showing who is in the lead. The example described below is based on Pictionary.

Picturing Chinese Technology

The example here on Chinese technology is easily adapted to explore the contribution of another culture or within a global context that includes multiple cultures. Prepare a deck of index cards or use some other method to list Chinese inventions and discoveries. Each card has the name and date of the invention or discovery.

Divide students into teams of four. A member of a team comes to the front of the class and draws a card. The student has 60 seconds to draw the invention or discovery but cannot talk or write letters or numbers. His teammates try to guess the invention or discovery. If their team members guess correctly within the time frame, their team earns a point. If they do not guess correctly, then other teams have 30 seconds to make a correct guess. If one of them guesses correctly, that team gains a point. If no one guesses, no teams earn a point, and the drawer reads the cards. The game continues in round-robin fashion for a set period of time.

After the game ends, debrief the activity. If more cards remain, the teacher can read them to the class. Discuss the inventions and discoveries to ensure students grasp the contributions made by the culture, in this case China, to our current-day society.

A short list of Chinese inventions and discoveries includes the items listed above. Other examples are paper (ca. 100 CE), movable type (ca. 1000 CE), mechanical clock (ca. 700 CE), seismograph (ca. 100 CE), paddle-wheel boat (ca. 400 CE), chemical warfare (ca. 300 BCE), spinning wheel (ca.1000 CE), kite (450 BCE), wheelbarrow (ca. 100 BCE), steel (ca. 100 BCE), and the canal lock (ca. 900 CE).[30]

A different game that serves a similar purpose is Jeopardy. Instead of cards, the teacher or students prepare answers related to technology categories such as transportation, communication, industry, agriculture, and everyday life. Teams of students raise their hand or use some other signal to pose questions for the answers. A round-robin format is also possible.

CONCLUSION

In many ways, world history presents the greatest challenge to teachers and students. How can the world be organized for effective teaching and learning? This chapter has explored various ideas on organizing world history for study and teaching, including organizing the subject by eras. We also have identified different approaches: chronological, thematic, and a hybrid of both. Classroom examples have been discussed that encompass multiple civilizations during a specific time period, using themes to connect past to present, and engaging activities such as games to motivate learning.

In one way or another, all the examples are based upon the triad of inquiry, primary sources, and literacy. Inquiry provides the organizational framework to manage the content so that it is of an appropriate scope and scale for student learning. Inquiry required students to define a classical age making the study of axial/classical age civilizations viable. Themes add another organizational level that focuses study on selected aspects of a topic. The axial/classical age example had four important themes: philosophy, religion, government, and technology. The theme of child labor facilitated connecting the past to the present.

This chapter showed how the combination of organizational ideas, the chronological/thematic approach, and the triad can transform the blank slate of world history into a viable subject for study. The next chapter takes on the challenge of doing the same thing for United States history.

NOTES

1. Chinese World Map. Groven's Sinocentrism, 2005. https://www.flickr.com/photos/kongharald/229645279.

2. "What Is the Prime Meridian—and Why Is It in Greenwich?" Royal Museums Greenwich, n.d. https://www.rmg.co.uk/stories/topics/what-prime-meridian-why-it-greenwich.

3. Jerry Bentley, *Shapes of World History in Twentieth-Century Scholarship* (Washington, DC: American Historical Association, 1996), 2. The following discussion on the historiography of world history is adapted from Bentley.

4. Marshall G. S. Hodgson, "Hemispheric Interregional History as an Approach in World History," in Ross Dunn (ed.), *The New World History: A Teacher's Companion* (Boston: Bedford/St. Martin's, 2000), 120–123.

5. Robert B. Marks, *The Origins of the Modern World: A Global and Environmental Narrative form the Fifteenth to the Twenty-First Century*, 4th edition (Lanham, Maryland: Roman & Littlefield, 2020); Peter Frankopan, *The Silk Roads: A New History the World* (New York: Vintage Book, 2015).

6. William H. McNeill, *A History of the Human Community: Prehistory to the Present*, 3rd edition (Englewood Cliff, New Jersey: Prentice Hall, 1990). See also William H. McNeill, *Plagues and Peoples* (New York: Anchor Books, 1976); William H. McNeill, *The Pursuit of Power: Technology, Armed Force, and Society since A.D. 1000*, 2nd edition (Chicago: University Chicago Press, 1984).

7. Linda Shaffer, "Southernization," in Ross Dunn (ed.), *The New World History: A Teacher's Companion* (Boston: Bedford/St. Martin's, 2000), 175–190. On technology, see for example. Daniel R. Headrick, *Technology: A World History* (New York: Oxford University Press, 2009); Arnold Pacey and Franseca Bray, *Technology in World Civilizations: A Thousand-Year History*, revised edition (Cambridge: MIT Press, 2021).

8. K. N. Chaudhuri, *Trade and Civilisation in the Indian Ocean: An Economic History from the Rise of Islam to 1750* (Cambridge, Great Britain: Cambridge University Press, 1985); Philip Curtin, *Cross Cultural Trade in World History* (New York: Cambridge University Press, 1984); David Christian, *Maps of Time: An Introduction to Big History* (Berkeley: University of California Press, 2004).

9. Alfred Crosby, *The Columbian Exchange: Biological and Cultural Consequence of 1492* (Westport, CT: Greenwood Press, 1973); Alfred Crosby, *Ecological Imperialism: The Biological Expansion of Europe, 900–1900* (New York: Cambridge University Press, 1986); Jared Diamond, *Guns, Germs, and Steel: The Fates of Human Societies* (New York: W. W. Norton, 1998); Jared Diamond, *Collapse: How Societies Choose to Fail or Succeed* (New York: Viking, 2005); Joachim Radkau, *Nature and Power: A Global History of the Environment* (New York: Cambridge University Press, 2008).

10. William A. Green, "Periodizing World History," in Ross Dunn (ed.), *The New World History: A Teacher's Companion* (Boston: Bedford/St. Martin's, 2000), 385.

11. Green, "Periodizing World History," 385.

12. The table is compiled from Christian, *Maps of Time*, 210; McNeill, *A History of the Human Community: Prehistory to the Present*, 3rd edition, iii–xi; Peter Stearns, "Periodization in World History Teaching: Identifying the Big Changes," in Dunn, *The New World History*, 364–376; Jerry Bentley, "Cross-Cultural Interaction and Periodization in World History," in Dunn, *The New World History*, 376–384; UCLA

National History Standards (Los Angeles: UCLA National Center for History in the Schools, 1996), https://phi.history.ucla.edu/nchs/world-history-content-standards/.

13. Stearns, "Periodization in World History Teachings," 364–376.

14. McNeill, *A History of the Human Community*, xv; Bentley, "Cross-Cultural Interaction and Periodization in World History," 377.

15. Anthony, F. C. Wallace, "Revitalization Movements," *American Anthropologist* 58, no. 2 (April 1956): 264–265.

16. Ibrahim Turan, "Thematic vs. Chronological History Teaching Debate: A Social Media Research," *Journal of Education and Learning* 9, no. 1 (January 2020): 206, 212.

17. Ibrahim, "Thematic vs. Chronological History Teaching Debate," 205, 210.

18. Ibrahim, "Thematic vs Chronological History Teaching Debate," 213.

19. Karl Jaspers, *The Origin and Goal of History* (New Haven, CT: Yale University Press, 1953), 1–22.

20. Hannah Droer, "Alone, Underage, and Exploited for Labor," *The New York Times,* February 26, 2023, pp. 1, 18–20.

21. Charles Booth, "Occupations of the People of the United Kingdom, 1801–81," *Journal of the Statistical Society of London* 49, no. 2 (June 1886): 314–444, 353, 357.

22. John C. Cobden, *The White Slaves of England*, Miller Orton & Mulligan (Auburn, England and Buffalo, New York: Miller Orton & Mulligan, 1854) title page.

23. Cobden, *The White Slaves of England*, 142.

24. Cobden, *The White Slaves of England*, 38.

25. Children's Employment Commission, *First Report of the Commissioners: Mines* (London: William Clowes and Sons, 1842), 77.

26. International Labour Office and United Nations Children's Fund, *Child Labour: Global Estimates 2020, Trends and the Road Forward* (ILO and UNICEF, New York, 2021), 21, 22, 38.

27. International Labour Office and United Nations Children's Fund, *Child Labour*, 61.

28. Droer, "Alone, Underage, and Exploited for Labor," 1.

29. Alfred Crosby, *Ecological Imperialism: The Biological Expansion of Europe, 900–1900*, 2nd edition (New York, Cambridge University Press, 2004), 104–131; Daniel R. Headrick, *Technology: A World History* (New York: Oxford University Press, 2009), 71–75.

30. Robert Temple, *The Genius of China: 3,000 Years of Science, Discovery, and Invention*, 3rd edition (London: Andre Deutsch, 2007).

Chapter 6

United States History

At the beginning of the school year in a United States history course up to 1865, major concerns include building community, orienting students to the class, and diagnosing student prior knowledge. One idea is to ask students in groups to analyze one of the visuals shown in Figure 6.1.[1] Ask each group to answer the following questions:

1. What type of document is this?
2. What does it show or say?
3. What does the document tell us about United States history before 1865?

Next, jigaw the groups so that each group includes a member from each of the original groups. After sharing their answers, ask each group to connect each of the documents to one of the following course themes: democracy, race and slavery, technology, and territorial expansion. Ask each group to record their answers on a graphic organizer such as Figure 6.1, writing the theme under the appropriate document.

After hearing and synthesizing the answers, close the activity with a whole class discussion. Ask students what they know about these themes in relation to U.S. history and to pose questions about these themes to use in the course.

The activity fulfills several needs at the beginning of a school year. It helps build a class community of learners through the group work collaboration. The teacher gets a sense of student prior knowledge and skills abilities, literacy and social-emotional. The students learn about the major themes of the course and experience what they will do over the school year. The students also learn that they are responsible for their own learning and that their voices and opinions are valued.

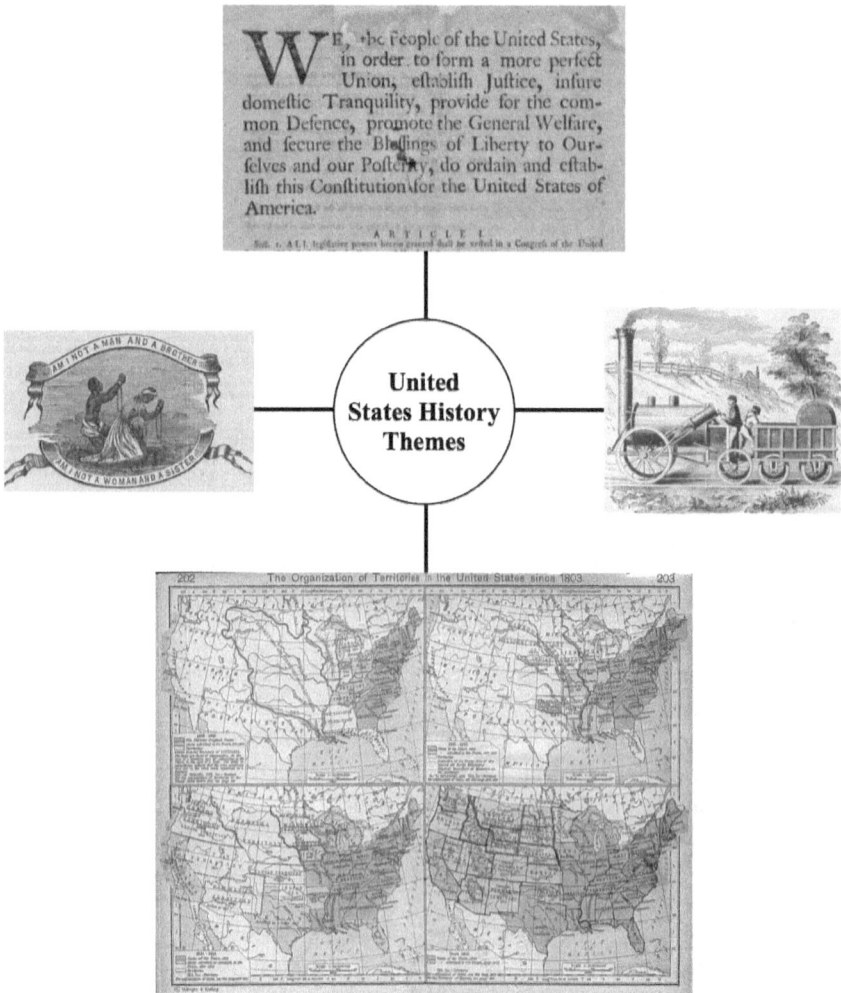

Figure 6.1. United States History Themes.

CHAPTER OVERVIEW

This chapter explores teaching and learning of United States history in Grades 6–12. The chapter answers three questions:

1. How can teaching and learning showcase the diverse master narratives that comprise United States history?
2. How can themes help students make connections between the past and the present?

3. How does the triad of inquiry-based learning, primary sources, and literacy make U.S. history come alive for middle and high school students?

STUDYING UNITED STATES HISTORY

An important consideration is that U.S. history has a different complexity than world history. Depending upon the approach, it often has a smaller time frame. The spatial context is more compact. While it does extend regionally, continentally, and globally, the focus is on the United States. The recurring culture wars over the teaching of U.S. history show the particular character of issues on inclusion, relevance, and the political state of the nation. The current culture war is as much a political football, especially among politicians, as a debate over a single master versus diverse narratives.

Similarities also exist between United States, world, and other fields of history. The same basic questions animate debate over the best ways to teach and the best ways to learn history:

1. What is the best way to organize history for study and for teaching and learning?
2. How do teachers accommodate large amounts of content so what students learn is inclusive and relevant?
3. How do teachers expand the historical content to be taught and learned so it coherently encompasses not just political but also cultural, economic, environmental, and social history?

Another fundamental query concerns how to integrate skills development with the learning of content.

The History of U.S. History

Over the last 80 years, various commissions and committees have wrestled with the issue of history education in the schools. Their reports are chapters in the history of U.S. history that provide content and context into current conditions. Three important studies are

- the 1944 Report on American History in Schools and Colleges,
- the 1989 Bradley Commission on History in the Schools, and
- the 1994 National Standards for United States History.

The studies had several similarities. All were collaborative efforts that included representatives of professional associations and/or other organizations, university faculty, and school representatives. Each identified the important role history plays in building competent citizens. All of the studies lamented the declining or poor state of history education in the schools. Each issued recommendations for Grade 6–12 U.S. history curricula. Compare the different curricula to those used in schools today to see how much has changed and how much has remained the same.

Report on American History in Schools and Colleges

In 1943, the American Historical Association, the Mississippi Valley Historical Association (later the Organization of American Historians), and the National Council for the Social Studies formed a committee to study American history in the schools and colleges. The 14-member committee included professors of history and education as well as two high school teachers.[2]

The committee issued its report in 1944. One finding was that while most Americans did not recall name and dates, they did understand trends and movements. Regarding methods of teaching and learning, the report said little behind noting students should learn the historical method. As for primary sources, the only mention was about ensuring students distinguish between primary and secondary sources.

According to the report, U.S. history was required by 45 states in elementary school and 46 states in high schools. In middle and junior schools, all students studied U.S. history, likely in grade 8. In high schools, nearly every student studied U.S. history in grades 9, 11, or 12.

The report also explained that societal changes affected the content of U.S. history courses. Three new emphases were identified: increased interest in social and economic forces, greater focus on the international setting, and enhanced study of the ideals and traditions of democracy. The report presented curriculum recommendations for middle, junior high, and senior high school that included major themes and skills for each level. Note that the time frames of the various levels overlapped but only in senior high school did students study the present day.

Middle Grades (4–6): How People Live, 1607–1850 included the following themes and skills:

- *Themes*: exploration of the hemisphere, types of colonial settlement, ways of living in the early English colonies of the Atlantic Seaboard, westward movement, immigration, and the map of North America
- *Skills*: using the table of contents, and the like, to locate information, acquiring basic vocabulary, reading simple maps, listing items and tracing simple sequences, and distinguishing between generalizations and specific statements

Junior High (7–9): The Building of the Nation, 1775–circa 1870 had the following themes and skills:

- *Themes*: the American Revolution; the rise of industrial Northeast, plantation South, and free-farm West; territorial development, the struggle over new states, and the Civil War; the development of waterways, highways, railways, and airways, and of domestic and international trade; recreation, sport, and social life; the rise and influence of major communication industries
- *Skills*: interpret visuals, study complex maps, outlining, locating library and other materials, making and critiquing generalizations, summarizing, and acquiring vocabulary

Senior High (10–12): A Democratic Nation in a World Setting, 1619–1939 included the following themes and skills:

- *Themes*: the development of the American political system, the growth of democracy, the growth of the American people, the second industrial revolution, the international influence and responsibilities of the United States, American ideas and ideals
- *Skills*: distinguishing between fact and opinion, distinguishing between primary and secondary sources, understanding people and events in their time and cultural context, participating in group discussions, note-taking, making inferences and generalizations, and reading different types of maps

The three-course sequence spanning Grades 4–12 followed a progressive sequence of learning. Overlapping time frames meant that students learned similar content in somewhat different contexts over time. They also developed skills progressively to higher levels of proficiency.

The Bradley Commission

The 1983 publication of *A Nation at Risk* that strongly criticized the state of U.S. education stimulated a wave of curricular reform movements. In 1987, the Bradley Foundation (Milwaukee, Wisconsin) established the Bradley Commission on History in the Schools, a 17-member body of historians and school teachers, chaired by historian Kenneth T. Jackson of Columbia University. Its purpose was to explore conditions affecting U.S. history in the schools and make recommendations. The commission emphasized curriculum not pedagogy, so methods were not explored. Little was said about primary sources.[3]

The report noted that the 11th-grade U.S. history course was no longer universal and that in middle schools area studies had replaced courses with historical content. Fifteen percent of American students did not study U.S. history in high school. Its recommendations included requiring all students to study history and that a minimum of four years of history education be required for Grades 7–12. The commission also suggested using a diverse narrative approach to history that included women, all racial and ethnic groups, and all economic classes.[4]

In keeping with its focus, the Bradley Commission paid close attention to curriculum, offering major themes, topics, and different curricular patterns. Six vital themes were identified: civilization, cultural diffusion, and innovation; human interaction with the environment; values, beliefs, political ideas, and institutions; conflict and cooperation; comparative history of major developments; and patterns of social and political interaction.

The commission identified eight topics as being central to U.S. history. They included the evolution of American political democracy, American economic development, the meeting of people and cultures from many nations, the changing role of the United States in the outside world, family and local history, and the changing character of American society and culture. The last two topics focused on issues relevant to the history wars: distinctively American tensions and the successes and failures of the United States.

Four curricular patterns were provided for middle and high school. All paired history with geography. Patterns A and B suggested teaching U.S. history and geography in Grades 8 and 11. Pattern C recommended teaching U.S. history and geography to 1914 in Grade 8 and the 20th century in Grade 11. Pattern D did not recommend teaching U.S. history and geography until high school and then followed a two-year sequence.[5]

Equally important, Jackson observed that the findings and recommendations were not the last word on history education in the schools. As it happens, several years later, in 1994, controversy erupted over the National Standards for United States History.

The National Standards for United States History

In 1994, the UCLA National Center for History in the Schools published its National Standards for History focusing on U.S. and world history content standards. Based on recommendations made by two panels of educators and teachers, the standards were revised in 1996. UCLA professors Gary B. Nash (history) and Charlotte Crabtree (education) directed the effort funded by the National Endowment of the Humanities and the U.S. Department of Education.[6]

A 30-member National Council for History Standards oversaw the development of the standards. Council members included past and present presidents of national history, social studies, and educational professional associations, representatives from city and county school districts, historians, and schoolteachers. Also serving were representatives from the National Assessment of Educational Progress (NAEP) and the Congressionally-mandated National Council for Education Standards and Testing.

In addition, a National Forum for History Standards was established. The forum was composed of representatives from education, public interest, parent-teacher, and other organizations concerned with history in the schools. The forum provided counsel on the standards. Other focus groups and curriculum task forces also contributed to the development of the standards. Despite the broad-based participation, the standards were roundly criticized by conservatives as part of the ongoing culture wars.

Both skills and content standards were developed. The standards have a separate section on historical thinking standards. Inquiry and primary source analysis were foundations of the thinking skills. Five historical thinking skills were highlighted: chronological thinking, historical comprehension, historical analysis and interpretation, historical research capabilities, and historical issues-analysis and decision making.

Regarding content, U.S. history was organized into ten eras with overlapping time frames for Grades 5–12: three worlds meet (beginnings to 1620), colonization and settlement (1585–1763), revolution and the new nation (1754–1820s), expansion and reform (1801–1861), Civil War and Reconstruction (1850–1877), development of the industrial United States (1870–1900), emergence of modern America (1870–1930), the Great Depression and World War II (1929–1945), postwar United States (1945–early 1970s), and contemporary United States (1968–present).

In part due to the controversy over the standards, they have exerted a strong influence on history education. The debate over the standards stimulated public interest in history education leading to widespread dissemination of the standards and greater recognition of the value of a history education. Many states have used the standards to develop their own standards.

History of U.S. History in Perspective

The different reports of the last 80 years exemplify the historical theme of change and continuity. The goals of history education and the concerns over the status of history in the school curriculum remain unchanged. While wording may differ, many themes and topics are similar. Differences also are evident. Reflecting societal change and the emergence of different ideas, the Bradley Commission and the National Standards for U.S. History integrate diverse narratives into the history curriculum. They also highlight studying controversial issues of U.S. successes and failures.

The following sections explore different examples of diverse narratives that can be integrated into the classroom. They apply the triad by inquiring into how different groups responded to the impact of historical events, movements, and trends. Primary source analysis and building literacy skills are core learning components.

INDIGENOUS AMERICANS AND THE AMERICAN REVOLUTION

Traditionally, from the perspective of the United States, the American Revolution is a story of liberation from an oppressor followed by union into a new nation. A different narrative describes the experience of many of the over 250,000 indigenous people in 80 tribes and confederacies living east of the Mississippi River in 1776.[7] Virtually all of them were involved in the conflict.

The split between patriots and loyalists reflected a similar divide in indigenous American communities. For European Americans, the revolution was either a war for liberty to create a new nation or treason. Indigenous peoples allied with one side or the other. But in the end, the revolution was another instance where the indigenous groups lost their freedom and unions were torn asunder. As some indigenous leaders explained to the Spanish governor Cruzat in St. Louis in 1784, "[t]he event was for us the greatest blow that could have been dealt us, unless it had been our total destruction."[8]

The American Revolution opened a new chapter for indigenous Americans. Prior to the revolution, various peoples, including the Iroquois and Cherokee, had practiced balance of power diplomacy. Until the French-Indian War removed the French and Spanish from the eastern United States, indigenous people played European powers against each other. After 1763, the Iroquois and Cherokee pursued a similar policy with the British and the colonists. The U.S. victory in the revolution eliminated their ability to engage in balance of power diplomacy. A telling point is that the 1783 Treaty of Paris did not include indigenous representatives.

Teachers can easily integrate the story of the indigenous people into the study of the American Revolution. Numerous resources exist. The National Endowment for the Humanities EDSITEment web site has an excellent lesson plan on the role of indigenous Americans in the revolution (https://edsitement.neh.gov/lesson-plans/native-americans-role-american-revolution-choosing-sides). There also are various internet sites that have print documents related to the indigenous experience during the revolution.[9]

The Iroquois in the American Revolution

The diverse narrative of the Iroquois offers insight into the impact the revolution had on indigenous people. Initially, as tensions increased between the patriots and the British, the six tribes comprising the Iroquois Confederacy (Seneca, Cayuga, Onondaga, Oneida, Mohawk, and Tuscarora) adopted a position of neutrality. On June 19, 1775, the Oneida sent a transcript of a speech to Connecticut governor Trumbull to be communicated to the Continental Congress:

> Brothers: Possess your minds in peace respecting us Indians. We cannot intermeddle in the dispute between two brothers. The quarrel seems to be unnatural. You are two brothers of one blood. We are unwilling to join on either side in such a contest, for we bear an equal affection to both of you Old and New England. . . . The present situation of you two brothers is new and strange to us. We Indians cannot find, nor recollect in our traditions of our ancestors, the like case, or a similar instance.[10]

The Continental Congress replied on July 13, 1775, sending a message to all six tribes in the Iroquois Confederacy. The message also requested neutrality. "This is a family quarrel between us and Old England," the message stated, noting that "[y]ou Indians are not concerned in it. We don't wish you to take up the hatchet against the king's troops. We desire you to remain at home, and not join on either side, but keep the hatchet buried deep."[11]

Unfortunately, over time, many indigenous groups became embroiled in the war on both sides. The conflict split the Iroquois confederacy. Mohawks, Onondagas, Cayugas, and Seneca supported the British. The Oneida and Tuscarora backed the United States.

The Battle of Oriskany and Its Aftermath

An important breaking point was the Battle of Oriskany that occurred in upstate New York on August 6, 1777. It was a major engagement of the campaign that ended with the defeat of British General Burgoyne at Saratoga on October 17, 1777.[12] The inclusion of the Iroquois is generally noted in discussions of the Battle of Oriskany. The important role the Iroquois played on both sides and the impact the battle had on them is often omitted.

The Battle of Oriskany involved two armies consisting almost totally of participants from North America. A British loyalist and Iroquois army led by British General Barrimore St. Leger and Joseph Brant, a Mohawk leader, were attempting to capture Fort Stanwix. A joint patriot militia-Oneida army led by General Nicholas Herkimer and Han Yerry, an Oneida chief, were sent to keep the fort in Patriot hands. An 1857 recreation of the battle is shown in Figure 6.2 below.[13]

The engraving shows pitched fighting between Iroquois and Anglo soldiers in what was one of the bloodiest confrontations of the war. Estimates suggest the patriot forces lost 50% of their men, while the British lost 15%. Iroquois losses were calculated at 69 warriors and 23 war chiefs. Not surprisingly, the Oriskany battlefield is considered "a place of great sadness."[14]

Ultimately, neither side emerged a clear victor. The British retreated but eventually captured the fort. From the perspective of the Iroquois, the battle was the beginning of a civil war that ended the Iroquois confederacy. After the battle, the Iroquois aligned with the British sent a war hatchet, representing a formal declaration of war, to the Oneida. The inter-tribal conflict continued until 1779, when U.S. forces devastated the area known as Iroquoia.[15]

The American Revolution effectively ended the Iroquois confederacy that had lasted centuries. In subsequent years, through various treaties, the Iroquois lost most of their original lands. Many were forced to abandon their old ways of living to accommodate the new reality of being part of the United States.

Despite the destruction of their confederacy and the loss of land, not all of their traditions or culture were lost. In *The Iroquois in the American Revolution*, Barbara Graymont explained that the Iroquois retained their

Figure 6.2. Battle of Oriskany State of New York.

confederacy government led by heredity sachems. They also maintained their Longhouse religion, experiencing a revitalization in 1779 due to the preaching of the sachem Ganiodaio (Handsome Lake).[16]

Classroom Applications

Integrating the experience of the Iroquois into the study of the American Revolution offers students an opportunity to inquire into a neglected chapter of the war for independence. A selection of documents, including some of those included above, can be used for a documents-based questions (DBQ) lesson. Students might engage in role plays as Iroquois leaders to debate the question "Why did the Iroquois participate in the American Revolution?" A corollary question is "Why did the various members of the Iroquois confederacy choose one side or the other?"

The DBQ or role-play can be adapted for use to explore the experiences of other groups during the revolution or other conflicts. Students could participate in a mock trial, perhaps judging President Andrew Jackson's actions regarding Indian removal in the 1830s. Another option would be a research project. No matter what activity is selected, a pivotal event in U.S. history is studied from the perspective of a people whose story is seldom fully told in U.S. history courses.

AFRICAN AMERICAN FARMERS, 1865–CA. 1900

The end of the Civil War meant that the vast majority of African Americans faced a new reality. They were no longer enslaved. Freedom presented opportunities and posed challenges. Most instruction focuses on political and possibly educational improvements during Reconstruction, the rise of farm tenancy, and the segregation and the racism African Americans faced in the late 19th century. Without discounting the impact of racism on African Americans, a less-told story examines the responses of African American farmers to the conditions they faced during this period.

The African American Farmer in the South

Despite rumors of land distribution, the "forty acres and a mule" slogan, southern whites largely retained their property, especially in cleared, fertile areas. In rare situations, land was given to African Americans, but the recipients faced dire conditions.

James Lucas was an ex-enslaved person of the Confederacy president Jefferson Davis and others. In his 1930s Works Progress Administration

(WPA) interview, Lucas explained that because he had enlisted in the Union Army, after the war he received 160 acres of land in the Mound Bayou, Arkansas, area. But he had to live on the land to retain the title. The property was low and swampy. Lucas had no money or tools to drain the swamp, clear the land, and build a house. He lost the land and worked as a sharecropper.[17]

Before examining the conditions African American tenant farmers faced, let's look at the scope and scale of tenancy. As was the case with Lucas, the vast majority of African Americans worked in agriculture as tenant farmers or sharecroppers. In 1906, the U.S. Bureau of the Census published a report by W. E. B. DuBois titled "The Negro Farmer." According to DuBois, in 1900, African American farmers operated 746,717 farms that contained over 38 million acres and had a total value of almost $500 million. In 1900, 74.6% or 557,174 of the farms were operated by African American tenants.[18]

Conditions under Farm Tenancy

White landowners rented or provided land and housing to African American families. They supplied food, tools, seed, animals, and other supplies on credit, or furnish, as it was called. As had been true before the Civil War, after 1865, much of southern agriculture was a commercial endeavor focusing on the cultivation of a single staple crop for market, mostly cotton.

Numerous risks were connected to growing cotton. All involved, both white landowners and African American farmers had to cope with the vagaries of weather, pests as such as the boll weevil, and boom-and-bust market cycles, among other things. In 1930, Mississippi delta blue singer Edward James "Son" House recorded "Dry Spell Blues Parts 1 and 2" for Paramount Records. The lyrics described the hard times caused by drought:

> Now the people down south sure won't have no home
>
> Now the people down south sure won't have no home
>
> Because the dry spell have parched all this cotton and corn

A later lyric complained about market conditions and prices: "Pork chops forty-five cents a pound cotton is only ten."[19]

African American farmers contended with other challenges. The furnish meant that they started the year in the red. In part because they had no other choice, tenants bought supplies and other items on credit at the plantation or another store. Depending on the character of the owner, often the landowner, they paid fair or exorbitant prices for low quality goods. Many tenants also suffered from fraudulent bookkeeping. The result was that they accumulated more debt over the growing season.

At the end of the year, after the crop was harvested and sold, the African American farmers received their share of the crop. In good years, when a profit was made that paid off the debt, the sharecropper received some of the profits. In bad years, many African Americans were unable to pay off the debt. It was carried over to the following year, possibly miring the farmer in debt peonage.

Just how much cotton did African American farmers have to produce to pay their debts? While the amount varied, in 1883, *Scribner's Monthly* published an article on the Barrow plantation in Georgia that reported each family farmed between 25–30 acres. Half was planted in cotton, the cash crop, and the rest in corn and small plots of potatoes, melons, and possibly other vegetables. In 1883, each farmer needed to harvest 750 pounds of cotton to pay the rent.[20]

The harsh conditions and the vagaries of cotton culture meant that the vast majority of African American farm families lived in poverty. Typically, their homes were two-room ramshackle wooden cabins. They supplemented their diets with corn, potatoes, and vegetables grown in garden plots. Children may or may not have attended school. If they did go to school, often work on the farm took precedence. Not surprisingly, many African American farmers responded to these conditions by seeking improvement.

African American Farmer Responses to Post-Civil War Conditions

The end of enslaved status meant that African American farmers had some control over their lives. African Americans exercised their newfound freedom in three major areas:

1. Type of work and the location of their residence
2. Ability to move
3. Farm ownership

Changes in Work and Residence

Major changes in work and life occurred because African American farmers rejected the pre–Civil War gang system of work, influencing the rise of tenancy. Two maps of the Barrow plantation from 1860 and 1880 (Figure 6.3) illustrate the changes that occurred because tenancy allowed many to choose where they lived and worked.[21]

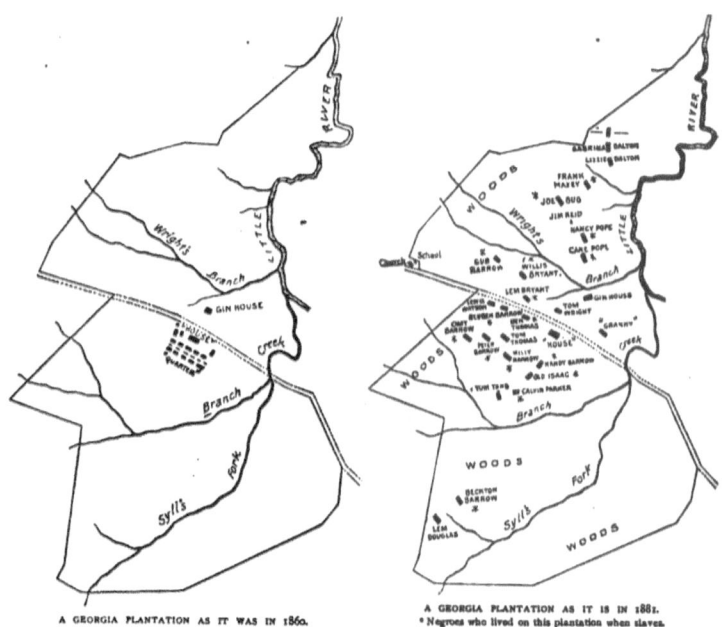

Figure 6.3. Barrow Plantation from 1800 and 1860. David C. Barrow Jr., "A Georgia Planation," *Scribner's Monthly* 21, no. 5 (March 1881): 833.

The 1860 map shows that before the Civil War, African Americans lived clustered around the landowner's house to facilitate close supervision. They did not order their day. They were told when, where, and how to work. Everyone labored together in the gang system in the fields or in the house.

The 1880 map depicts a very different situation. Depending upon the contract with the landowner, each family farmed their own plot. Many African American farmers chose where they lived on the plantation. Few selected plots near the landowner's house. Some chose remote areas to lessen contact with the landowner and likely other white people. As long as enough cotton was planted to pay the rent, the farmers were free to sow other corps and raise animals without much supervision. Families did not fear being separated.

Freedom to Move

James Lucas also noted a significant difference between being enslaved and being free, "One ob de rights ob bein free was dat we could move around en change bosses."[22] Mobility was an incredibly important freedom African Americans gained after the Civil War. It involved much more than changing bosses. Most African American movement before 1900 was internal in the South, often to newly opened lands that offered greater economic promise.

Some African Americans migrated into cities. An omen of the future occurred in the 1870s when thousands of African Americans left the South for Kansas.

The Exodusters

The end of Reconstruction and the withdrawal of Union troops from the South signaled a massive change for African Americans. Southerners regained control of the region. Racism increased culminating in the 1890 Mississippi state constitution and the 1896 Supreme Court decision in *Plessy v. Ferguson* that legalized segregation. Worsening conditions increased African American discontent.

Benjamin "Pap" Singleton was an ex-enslaved person from Tennessee who bought land in Kansas in 1869. Throughout the 1870s, using promotional handbills such as Figure 6.4 below, he helped African Americans move to Kansas. The 1878 election in Louisiana prompted what became known as the "Great Exodus" to Kansas in 1879. Over 6,000 African Americans known as Exodusters migrated from Mississippi, Louisiana, and other southern states to Kansas. In total, during the 1870s and early 1880s, over 20,000 African Americans moved to Kansas, but many faced great hardships.[23]

The "Ho For Kansas!" handbill was one of many fliers and posters that called for southern African Americans to move to Kansas. Addressing the message to "Brethren Friends, and Fellow Citizens" creates a sense of familiarity and community. The flier highlights that the writer is a friend, identifying Singleton as "Old Pap." He is thankful to inform the reader of the opportunity to pursue homes in the southwest, though actually it was Kansas. Cheap transportation rates are touted as is a warning to beware of speculators. Another personal touch was that those seeking more information could call on Singleton at his Nashville address.

Given the large number of migrants, Singleton's message was warmly welcomed. The migration to Kansas became the first large movement of African Americans out of the South. Especially at the turn of the 20th century, African American migration north increased, culminating in the Great Migration that began in 1914 and continued for decades.

The African American Farm Owner

In "The Negro Farmer," DuBois noted a significant sign of progress. One in four African American farmers in the South owned their land. Given that African American farm ownership in 1865 was virtually nonexistent, the fact that 25% had risen to be landowners was remarkable.

In the South, the percentage of African American landownership was highest in West Virginia (72%). Other states above 25% included, in descending

Ho for Kansas!

Brethren, Friends, & Fellow Citizens:

I feel thankful to inform you that the

REAL ESTATE AND Homestead Association,

Will Leave Here the

15th of April, 1878,

In pursuit of Homes in the Southwestern Lands of America, at Transportation Rates, cheaper than ever was known before.

For full information inquire of

Benj. Singleton, better known as old Pap,

NO. 5 NORTH FRONT STREET.

Beware of Speculators and Adventurers, as it is a dangerous thing to fall in their hands.

Nashville, Tenn., March 18, 1878.

One of the many posters calling on southern blacks to leave for Kansas.

Figure 6.4. "Ho for Kansas."

order, Oklahoma, Virginia, Maryland, Indian territory, Florida, Kentucky, Delaware, North Carolina, Texas, the District of Columbia, and Tennessee. The lowest percentages were, in descending order, Arkansas, South Carolina, Mississippi, Louisiana, Alabama, and Georgia (13.7%).

Percentages tell one story, but numbers tell another. The largest number of African American farm owners were in Virginia (26,566), Mississippi (21,973), and Texas (20,139); while the lowest number were in Delaware (332) and the District of Columbia (5). DuBois explained that moving to new lands in Mississippi and Texas was a major reason why those states had high ownership figures.[24]

In the study of Africans after the Civil War, students seldom examine the progress made in the face of harsh, deteriorating conditions. Yet, as the discussion on residence and type of work, movement, and land ownership show, African Americans consistently worked to better their situation. These efforts and others are pivotal chapters in the African American diverse narrative. How can they be integrated into an already crowded curriculum?

Classroom Applications

All the usual suspects can be used to help students learn about African American progress between 1865 and circa 1900. DBQs, research projects, role plays or other simulations, and presentations of various sorts are excellent activities that engage students in inquiry and primary source analysis to build literacy skills. Perhaps, the most important aspect is how the experience is approached.

The undeniable fact is that African Americans faced an incredible array of harsh conditions during this time period. Most started in abject poverty, and many remained in that state throughout their lives. Every day, they confronted racism often accompanied by violence. Segregation was really separate but unequal. Human and environmental forces made farming a risky business at best.

The question students should answer is not "What conditions did African Americans face between 1865 and 1900?" Instead, the question is "How and why did African Americans respond to the conditions that they faced?" The conditions are the starting point. The responses are the meat of the study.

The three examples discussed above show that African Americans resisted the harsh conditions in several ways, achieving some progress. The gang labor system and residential clustering to maintain tight control of behavior gave way to independent family farmers often living far from the landowner's house. Movement provided freedom to seek better employment or to escape to hopefully better living conditions. Both independent farming and mobility contributed to the freedom of sorts that came from owning your farm.

By taking the approach of stressing responses to conditions, a fuller, more robust study occurs. Students can examine cause, effect, and response to various conditions. They can examine the racial, economic, political, and environmental conditions the African American farmers faced to assess the effects these things had on their lives and their work. Next, they study the various responses to these causes and effects.

As a classroom topic, the African American farmer experience is an important story in the diverse narrative of African American and U.S. history. Its ramifications are still playing out today.

DIVERSE NARRATIVES OF WORLD WAR II

As is true of virtually all nations, war has been an unfortunate, recurring experience of United States history. World War II is a special category for several reasons, including the truly global nature of the conflict and also the use of nuclear weapons. Another distinction is that the United States purportedly fought to secure four essential freedoms for every person in the world. In his inaugural address on January 6, 1941, President Franklin D. Roosevelt proclaimed what would become four major war aims:

1. Freedom of speech and expression
2. Freedom for every person to worship God in his own way
3. Freedom from want that meant securing a healthy peace time
4. Freedom from fear of war

Roosevelt also described the foundations of a healthy democracy that would help realize these freedoms. The list included equality of opportunity, jobs, security, ending of special privilege for the few, preservation of civil liberties for everyone, and a rising standard of living.[25]

World War II created dilemmas and opportunities for members of certain races, ethnic groups, and religions. In 1942, the *Pittsburgh Courier*, an African American newspaper, coined a slogan that probably resonated with many other groups. The Double V, or Double Victory, campaign sought to achieve military victory over fascism and to win equal rights at home. The slogan symbolized the contradiction between the war aims and Roosevelt's Four Freedoms abroad versus the racism, antisemitism and sexism that prevailed in the United States

Conditions on the Home Front

Prior to and during the war, African Americans, Asian Americans, Jewish Americans, Mexican Americans, indigenous people, and women lived under unequal conditions. They often confronted hostile, at times violent, situations. The war raised serious questions about supporting the conflict.[26] On one hand, it offered an opportunity to show their patriotism and secure equal conditions. On the other hand, participation in World War I had not led to many gains.

African Americans

Segregation and racial violence characterized African American life. In 1940 as the United States geared up for war, African Americans were blocked by segregation from securing jobs in war industries. Civil rights leader A. Philip Randolph organized a march on Washington DC to protest against job discrimination forcing President Roosevelt to issue an executive order banning discrimination by race, color, creed, or national origin. African Americans gained employment but worked under segregated conditions. They were paid less, given menial jobs, not allowed to advance, entered work in separate doors, and had separate facilities.

Asian Americans

Asian Americans also lived under unequal conditions. They were largely excluded from immigrating to the United States and often lived in designated ethnic enclaves. Many Chinese Americans were confined to working in restaurants and laundries. In California, Asian Americans were not allowed to own land. After the United States entered the conflict, as discussed in Chapter 4, Japanese Americans were incarcerated in internment camps.

Jewish Americans

Jewish Americans confronted antisemitism before and during the war. Antisemitism was rampant in the 1930s. In 1938 and 1940, public opinion polls showed that almost two of every three Americans found Jews objectionable, and 50% thought German antisemitism was due to action by German Jews. In addition, Jews faced quotas in many universities and medical schools. They had restricted employment opportunities in engineering, insurance, and banking. Isolationists blamed war mobilization on Jews. Despite news of Hitler's violence and extermination campaign, Jews were barred from immigrating to the United States.[27]

Mexican Americans

Mexican Americans also faced discrimination and violent attacks. Most lived in clustered neighborhoods called barrios. They often attended segregated schools and did not have equal access to public places. Perhaps, the most glaring incident were the zoot suit riots in Los Angeles from June 3 to June 8, 1943. The violent clashes occurred between white servicemen and primarily Mexican American young men wearing zoot suits, a fashion trend of the time. Zoot suits featured loose fitting, long suit jackets with padded shoulders and wide lapels and baggy, cuffed trousers, hats, and long glittering watch chains.

In California, the clothes gained a racist connotation. Whites viewed the Mexican Americans zoot suitors as gang members, thugs, and juvenile delinquents. In reality, many zoot suiters were fans of jitterbug dancing while others wore the clothing to highlight a generational divide between young people and adults. A third group did engage in destructive behavior.

The zoot suit riots occurred between June 3 and June 8, 1943. Soldiers and sailors attacked young Mexican and other Americans wearing zoot suits, beating them and stripping them of their clothes. An estimated 100 Mexican Americans suffered serious injuries compared to 15 military personnel.[28]

Indigenous Americans

Having endured centuries of mistreatment, war, decimation by European diseases, and confinement for many on reservations, indigenous Americans often asked why they should fight a white man's war. Government policies had wreaked havoc on their culture and society leading to greater poverty and loss of land. The Indian Reorganization Act of 1934 sought to redress many of these grievances but had limited effect.

Women

The focus here is on white women since those belonging to racial, ethnic, and religious groups experienced the conditions described above. Traditionally, married women were the homemakers. For many, their domain was the house while their husbands took care of the outside affairs including making a living. Single and married women in the workplace were paid lower wages, blocked from advancement, and could suffer sexual harassment.

THE WAR AND OPPORTUNITY

U.S. entry into World War II brought great changes to U.S. society and opened opportunities for members of various groups. Two quotes sum up the feelings of many people. Alex Romania, a Mexican American stunt man in Hollywood explained, "Our country had been attacked and we had to defend it." But he also added, "All of us had to prove ourselves—to show that we were more American than the Anglos." An African American soldier added an important rationale for supporting war, stating, "I am a Negro soldier 22 years old. I won't fight or die in vain. If I fight, suffer, or die, it will be for the freedom of every black man to live equally with other races."[29]

The war provided opportunities for members of all groups. Either voluntarily or by being drafted, they served in the military, often with distinction. On the home front, they contributed to the war effort by working in industries and other fields in jobs that previously may not have been available to them. Military service is examined in the following section, starting with a basic question: who served in the armed forces during World War II?

Who Served in the Military during World War II?

Approximately 16.5 million Americans served in the military to secure the Four Freedoms and maintain democracy. Table 6.1 breaks down who served in the military by race, ethnicity, and gender.[30]

Table 6.1 shows that military service reflected the diversity of the United States The total population figures include those too young and too old to serve as well as people who were considered unable to serve for physical or other reasons. People unwilling to serve due to religious or other reasons

Table 6.1.

Group	Total U.S. Population (1940)	Number Served in Military	Approximate Percentage of Population Served in Military
Total U.S. Population	132,164,568	16,500,000	12.5
African Americans	14,100,000	901,896	6.3
Jewish Americans	4,800,000	550,000	11.5
Latinx Americans (Puerto Rican, Mexican)	1,600,000 (Based on Spanish speakers)	500,000	31
Women	65,770,000	350,000	.5–.6
Japanese Americans	120,000	33,000	27.5
Indigenous Americans	400,000	20,000	5
Chinese Americans	107,000 (40% not citizens)	13,311	13
Filipino Americans	45,563 in U.S.	11,506	35
Hawaiian	64,310	2,194	3.5

also are in the total figures. Another caveat is that the table does not include people who were serving the war effort at home by working in industry and other fields. An important point is that the draft played the major role in the number of Americans who served.

The numbers and percentages tell interesting stories. African Americans had the largest population and by far the greatest number in the military, but the percentage serving ranked seventh out of the ten groups in the table. African Americans also served in segregated units often led by white officers. The other groups who served in separate units were women, Japanese, and Filipinos. Chinese Americans were largely integrated into the armed services.[31] Almost one in three Mexican American and Puerto Ricans served in the military. They were integrated into the armed forces.

Beyond the numbers, telling the story of the military contributions made to the war effort is beyond the scope of this book. Every group contributed mightily to the success on the battlefield, earning numerous honors and citations. One effort that has received some notice but not regarding its full impact on the war effort is language diversity.

Language Diversity and the War Effort

Because they spoke English and Navajo well, the Navajo code talkers are the most famous examples of how language diversity contributed to military success. The Japanese could not understand or mimic Navajo. The 420 Navajo code talkers transmitted radio messages in their native language in battles in the Pacific theater of war from Guadalcanal to Okinawa.

Code talking was not the only way language diversity helped the U.S. military. Japanese Americans performed several functions. They intercepted and translated Japanese communications. They also interrogated Japanese prisoners of war.

On the battlefield, Japanese American soldiers performed other duties. In Chapter 4, Ray Matusmoto described how he infiltrated a Japanese camp and reported back on their attack plans. U.S. troops set up an ambush and when Japanese soldiers hesitated to advance, Matsumoto stood up, and in Japanese, ordered the soldiers to attack, which they did. The siege was broken, and U.S. reinforcements arrived to win the battle.[32]

An interesting experience involved Mexican American Guy Gabaldan, who spoke fluent Japanese. His first combat occurred during the battle of Saipan. Gabaldan went out alone and captured six Japanese soldiers. He sent three back to their camp to convince the others to surrender since they were surrounded. His efforts led to 800 Japanese soldiers surrendering. He received the Navy Cross for his actions.

Another group whose language diversity proved valuable were German and Austrian-Jewish soldiers. Many were members of the Ritchie Boys project that trained Jewish Americans to interrogate German prisoner of wars, among other things. Some were embedded with captured German soldiers in prisoner of war camps to gather information on any escape attempts.[33]

Regarding women, they performed essential services on and off the battlefield. In combat zones and other places, women served as nurses. Off the battlefield, they drove trucks, repaired airplanes, served as radio operators, flew military aircraft across the country, and worked as lab technicians.

The myriad experiences of members of various groups during World War II comprise numerous diverse narratives that show how often their members served the nation. There are great stories that are relatively easy to integrate into World War II instructional units. Whether it be for other wars or other movements, the discussion above is a model for students to learn the diverse narratives so that U.S. history becomes their story.

Classroom Activities

Numerous classroom scenarios from research projects to DBQs to writing diaries exist that engage students in exploring the diverse narratives of World War II. Another option is to have students engage in a simulation where students act as a government commission to evaluate the experiences of the diverse peoples of the United States during World War II. Students assume the personalities of commission members, representatives of various groups, and, perhaps, journalists covering the proceedings.

Each participating group has a specific task. Commission members write a report. Group representatives research and present experiences of their specific group. Journalists write editorials, news stories, create cartoons, and bring their work together in a publication or video newscast.

CONCLUSION

Because it is the history of the country they live in, United States history offers unique opportunities for teachers to engage students in conducting inquiry. Vast and deep collections of primary sources often accompanied by suggested classroom activities, are easily accessible. This chapter stressed diverse narratives that provide opportunities to develop culturally relevant and inclusive teaching and learning. The next and final chapter brings history even closer to home by examining how to integrate the local community in Grades 6–12 history education.

NOTES

1. "We the people of the United States, in order to form a more perfect union, establish justice, insure domestic tranquility, provide for the common defence, promote the general welfare, and secure the blessings of liberty to ourselves and our posterity, do ordain and establish this constitution for the United States of America," Dunlap and Claypoole (1787). Library of Congress Rare Book and Special Collections Division, http://hdl.loc.gov/loc.rbc/bdsdcc.n003001; U.S. Expansion since 1803, Wikimedia Commons, https://commons.wikimedia.org/wiki/File:USA_Expansion_since_1803.jpg; "Locomotive of 1828," in Albert S. Bolles, *Industrial History the United States, from Earliest Settlements to the Present Time* (Norwich, CT: The Henry Bill Publishing Company, 1878), 620. Internet Archive Book, https://archive.org/details/industrialhistor00boll/page/620/mode/1up?view=theater; Am I Not a Man and a Brother? Am I Not a Woman and a Sister?" Wikimedia Commons, https://commons.wikimedia.org/wiki/File:Am_I_not_a_man_and_a_brother%3F_Am_I_not_a_woman_and_a_sister%3F.jpg.

2. Edgar B. Wesley, *The Report of the Committee of American History in Schools and Colleges* (New York: The Macmillan Company, 1944). An unpaginated copy of the report is located on the American Historical Association web site. All information is taken from this report: https://www.historians.org/about-aha-and-membership/aha-history-and-archives/historical-archives/american-history-in-schools-and-colleges-(1944).

3. The Bradley Commission on History in Schools, "Building a History Curriculum: Guidelines for Teaching History in Schools," in Paul Gagnon and the Bradley Commission on History in Schools, *Historical Literacy: The Case for History in American Education* (Boston: Houghton Mifflin Company, 1989), 18.

4. Bradley Commission on History in Schools, "Building a History Curriculum," 16, 24.

5. Bradley Commission on History in Schools, "Building a History Curriculum," 27–39.

6. Gary B. Nash and Charlotte Crabtree (eds.), *History Standards* (online edition) (Los Angeles: National Center for History in the Schools, 1996). UCLA Public History Initiative, https://phi.history.ucla.edu/nchs/history-standards/. Unless otherwise noted, all information comes from this unpaginated online edition.

7. "Big Idea 5: Native American Soldiers and Scouts," Museum of the American Revolution, n.d., https://www.amrevmuseum.org/big-idea-5-native-american-soldiers-and-scouts.

8. Colin G. Calloway (ed.), *The World Turned Upside Down: Indian Voices from Early America* (New York: Bedford of St. Martin's Press, 1994), 146.

9. In addition to the sources cited above and EDSITEment, see the "Journals of the Continental Congress—Speech to the Six Nations," the Avalon Project: Documents in Law, History, and Diplomacy, Yale Law School, Lillian Goldman Law Library, https://avalon.law.yale.edu/18th_century/contcong_07-13-75.asp.

10. Peter Force (ed.), *Peter Force's Documentary History of the Early Days of the United States: American Archives,* 4th series, vol. 2 (Washington, DC: M. St. Clair Clarke and P. Force, 1836–1853), 1116–1117.

11. "Journals of the Continental Congress-Speech to the Six Nation, July 13, 1775" (New Haven: Goldman Law Library, Yale University, 2008), https://avalon.law.yale.edu/18th_century/contcong_07-13-75.asp.

12. Brady J. Crytzer, "Longhouse Lost: The Battle of Oriskany and the Iroquois Civil War," *Journal of the American Revolution* (July 30, 2020): https://allthingsliberty.com/2020/07/longhouse-lost-the-battle-of-oriskany-and-the-iroquois-civil-war/. Prior to the battle, Crytzer notes that disease had killed approximately 90 major chiefs of the Iroquois Confederacy, causing a leadership vacuum that broke up the confederacy.

13. John Reuben Chapin, *Battle of Oriskany, State of New York*, Ballou's pictorial, 12, no. 18 (May 2, 1857): 280. Library of Congress Prints and Photographs Division, https://hdl.loc.gov/loc.pnp/cph.3g12376.

14. Joy Bilharz, *Oriskany: A Place of Great Sadness* (Boston: Northeast Region Ethnography Program, National Park Service, 2009), 93; Crytzer, "Longhouse Lost."

15. Crytzer, "Longhouse Lost."

16. Graymont, Barbara, *The Iroquois in the American Revolution* (Syracuse, NY: Syracuse University Press, 1972), 293.

17. James Lucas, WPA Slave Narratives, MSGenWeb Library, http://msgw.org/slaves/lucas-xslave.htm.

18. W. E. B. DuBois, "The Negro Farmer," in *Negroes in the United States*, U.S. Bureau of the Census Bulletin no. 8 (Washington, D.C: U. S Bureau of the Census, 1904), 69, 78. An important point is that a farm was defined by who cultivated it: the owner, manager, or a tenant. A large plantation leased in smaller lots to 50 tenants was counted as 50 farms.

19. Son House, "Dry Spell Blues, Parts 1 and 2," Paramount (1930). Genius, https://genius.com/Son-house-dry-spell-blues-part-1-lyrics; https://genius.com/Son-house-dry-spell-blues-part-2-lyrics.

20. David C. Barrow Jr., "A Georgia Planation," *Scribner's Monthly* 21, no. 5 (March 1881): 833.

21. Barrow, "A Georgia Planation," 832–833.

22. James Lucas, WPA Slave Narratives.

23. "Ho For Kansas!" Copyprint of handbill, Historic American Building Survey Field Records, HABS FN-6, #KS-49 – 14. Prints and Photographs Division, Library of Congress (109), https://www.loc.gov/exhibits/african/images/hofokan.jpg.

24. W. E. B. DuBois, "The Negro Farmer," in *Negroes in the United States*, U.S. Bureau of the Census Bulletin no. 8 (Washington, DC: U. S Bureau of the Census, 1904), 81–82.

25. Franklin D. Roosevelt, address to Congress, January 6, 1941; First Carbon Files, Speeches of President Franklin D. Roosevelt, 1933–1945; Collection FDR-PPF: Papers as President, President's Personal File; Franklin D. Roosevelt Library, Hyde Park, NY. [Online Version, https://www.docsteach.org/documents/document/fdr-four-freedoms-speech, March 23, 2023], 10–11.

26. Ronald Takaki, *A Different Mirror: A History of Multicultural America*, review edition (New York: Back Bay Books), 350–358, offers good summaries of the experiences of various ethnic groups during World War II. Unless otherwise noted, the information on the home front comes from Takaki, 341–379.

27. Edward Shapiro, "World War II and American Jewish Identity," *Modern Judaism* 10, no. 1 (February 1990): 68–69.

28. Douglas Henry Daniels, "Los Angeles Zoot: Race 'Riot,' the Pachuco, and Black Music Culture," *The Journal of African American History* 87 (Winter 2002): 100.

29. Cited in Takaki, *A Different Mirror*, 351, 361–362.

30. "1940 Fast Facts," U. S Bureau of the Census (12/5/2022), https://www.census.gov/history/www/through_the_decades/fast_facts/1940_fast_facts.html; "1.2 Million Blacks Not Counted in 1940 Census, Records Reveal," *The Denver Post*, April 30, 2016, https://www.denverpost.com/2012/05/20/1-2-million-blacks-not-counted-in-1940-census-records-reveal/; "Total Jewish Population in the United States (1654–present)," Jewish Virtual Library (2023), https://www.jewishvirtuallibrary.org/jewish-population-in-the-united-states-nationally; "Why We Serve: Native Americans in the United States Armed Forces: World War II," National Museum of the American Indian (Washington, DC: Smithsonian Institution, 2020), https://americanindian.si.edu/static/why-we-serve/topics/world-war-2/; Economics and Statistics Administration, Bureau of the Census, *We The American . . . Hispanics* (Washington, DC: U.S. Department of Commerce, September 1992), 2; "Population of Chinese in the United States, 1860–1940 (48 Contiguous States Only)" (Urbana, IL: University of Illinois), http://teachingresources.atlas.illinois.edu/chinese_exp/resources/resource_2_9.pdf; "Table C-1. Asian and Pacific Islander, for the United States, Regions, Divisions, and States: 1990 (100-Percent Data)," Internet Archive Wayback Machine, https://web.archive.org/web/20100327164259/http://www.census.gov/population/www/documentation/twps0056/appC.pdf; Robert C. Schmitt, Demographic Statistics of Hawaii: 1778–1965. (Honolulu, 1968). United States. Bureau of the Census. 1970, 1980, 1990 Census of Population. General Population Characteristic (Washington, DC), United States. Bureau of the Census. Census 2000 Summary File 4 (SF 4) (April 29, 2003). Source: United States. Bureau of the Census. Census 2010 Summary File 1 (SF 1) (June 16, 2011).

31. Rudi Williams, "DoD's Personnel Chief Gives Asian-Pacific American History Lesson," Armed Forces Press Service: News Articles (June 3, 2005), U.S. Department of Defense, https://web.archive.org/web/20070615091238/http://www.defenselink.mil/news/newsarticle.aspx?id=16498.

32. See Chapter 4, pp. 80–83.

33. Jon Wertheim, "Ritchie Boys: The Secret U.S. Unit Bolstered by German-Born Jews Who Helped the Allies Beat Hitler," *CBS 60 Minutes*, originally broadcast July 3, 2002, https://www.cbsnews.com/news/ritchie-boys-60-minutes-2022-07-03/. The 60 minutes segment is an excellent overview of the Ritchie Boys.

Chapter 7

The Local Community

History is all around us. There is nothing like a walking tour (real or virtual) to show the truth of that statement. Imagine walking through tens of thousands of years of history but only traveling one and a half city blocks up a street, crossing to the other side, and retracing your steps to the starting point. Teachers, university faculty, and preservice teacher education candidates have taken such a tour in the park area of downtown Chicago, known familiarly as the city's front yard.

The tour starts on the southeast corner of Michigan Avenue and Monroe Street. Looking west, a formidable wall of concrete and steel high-rises line the east side of the street. Looking east, except for the Art Institute of Chicago, it is mostly park land to the shore of Lake Michigan a few blocks away. Why? Because in 1833 when the city was being laid out, four founding fathers had an idea. They designated a strip of land east of today's Michigan Avenue to be public land, forever free, and clear of permanent structures. It ran from Randolph Street in the north to what is now Roosevelt Road.

The forever, free, and clear mandate remains in place today, though it has been adapted to meet changing needs. Originally, all permanent structures were banned. In the 1890s, the building that became the Art Institute of Chicago was exempted, as were later additions to the museum. In the early 2000s, changing park design and public needs allowed permanent structures in Millennium Park including an outdoor concert venue. The same is true for Maggie Daley Park, which has playground equipment for children of different ages and an innovative ice-skating ribbon in the winter.

Walking east on the south side of Monroe Street to an overpass under which the Illinois Central Railroad tracks run offers an opportunity to span millennia of history. Tour guests are surprised to learn that if they were standing at the location 10,000 or so years ago, they would be under the ice of a glacier. As the glacier receded, it carved out the Great Lakes, meaning as late as the 1860s, the tour participants would be swimming in Lake Michigan.

In the 1850s, the Illinois Central Railroad was built on trestles out in the lake, helping Chicago become a railroad center. Resources and goods going east and west were funneled through Chicago. So were people, including European immigrants and later African American migrants from the South. Local history connected to major themes in U.S. and world history such as industrialization, railroads, immigration, and urban development, among others.

The big change happened after the Great Chicago Fire of 1871. There was no place to dispose of the remains from the fire that burned much of the central part of the city. The solution was to dump them in Lake Michigan, creating a landfill that moved the shoreline east. The landfills continued over time carving out the current shoreline that extends several city blocks east of the original shore.

Directing attention northwest to a tall building, tour participants learn it was the headquarters of the catalog pioneer Montgomery Ward, another connection to industrialization and also modernization. Along with Sears, Roebuck, and Company, Ward's catalog sold virtually everything a consumer could want by mail order, reaching into homes throughout the nation. Ward also liked looking out at the lakefront but, by the 1890s, the area had become a wasteland eyed by developers for building. Ward opposed building on the lakefront and launched a years-long lawsuit that ended in the early 1900s confirming the forever free and clear doctrine.

With the matter settled, park building began in Grant Park as it was called, after Ulysses S. Grant, Civil War hero and 18th president of the United States. Grant Park has walking and sitting areas, the famous Buckingham Fountain, tennis courts and ball fields, as well as gardens. It represents early 20th-century ideas on parks and recreation that favored open spaces.

The tour stops at the corner of Columbus Drive and Monroe Street, one block east of Michigan Avenue. Tour members see that its vast open spaces make Grant Park a likely venue for mass gatherings. Connections to U.S. history again emerge. Barack Obama's 2008 presidential election victory celebration was in Grant Park. Forty years earlier a few blocks south, during the 1968 Democratic Convention, anti–Vietnam War protesters clashed with police. The park hosts sports world championship celebrations, ethnic and music festivals, and Taste of Chicago. In summer 2023, Grant Park was at the center of a NASCAR cup series street race.

The tour moves to the north side of Monroe Street to preview two newer parks that reflect 21st-century ideas of park design. Where much of Grant Park is open space for large gatherings and allows visitors to create their own experiences, the newer parks feature interactive elements. Maggie Daley Park is the latest addition. Named after the late wife of former mayor Richard M. Daley, the park caters to children and has an ice-skating ribbon.

West of Columbus Drive, Millennium Park occupies 24.5 acres between Michigan Avenue and Columbus Drive and Monroe to Randolph Streets. The tour stops at the northwest corner of Columbus and Monroe to view a map of Millennium Park. Unlike Grant Park that was largely built with public funds, Millennium Park followed 21st-century practices, combining public and private funding. In return for their investment, private sponsors received naming rights.

Depending upon time, tour members either visit several attractions or hear short descriptions of them. One stop is Crown Fountain, an example of private funding. Crown Fountain is an interactive video sculpture consisting of two large glass block towers on opposite ends of a reflecting pool. The towers feature faces of Chicagoans spouting water into a large reflecting pool. Children and adults play in the waters during hot summer days.

Exiting the park and moving to the northeast corner of Michigan and Monroe, the tour ends. In approximately 45 minutes and over one and a half city blocks, tour members travel across millennia from the time of the glaciers to the present. Important aspects of Chicago history were noted, including many that connect local to national and world history. Tour members were introduced to city planning and park space, industrialization and the importance of the railroad, two different park designs, the 1968 Democratic Convention protests, and the 2008 presidential election. In addition, the use of parks for cultural events was highlighted.

The tour reinforces the idea that history has a local context connecting to national and possibly world history. Walking tours offer one option for integrating the local community into teaching and learning history. Numerous others exist.

CHAPTER OVERVIEW

This chapter explores bringing students closer to the history they study by integrating the local community into instruction. In this context, local community means areas smaller than large regions and states, such as neighborhoods, towns, villages, perhaps cities, suburbs, rural districts, and so on. The local connection could be a place, the built or natural environment, a person, groups of people, or events. This chapter seeks to answer three questions:

1. How can the local community be integrated into teaching and learning history?
2. Why is integrating the local community into teaching and learning history valuable?

3. How can the triad of inquiry, primary sources, and literacy help integrate study of the local community into teaching and learning history?

INTEGRATING THE LOCAL COMMUNITY INTO HISTORY TEACHING AND LEARNING

Because few middle and high schools offer local community courses, the connection needs to be made to a U.S. or world history course. The local is an example of a larger U.S. or world history topic or theme.

Two options exist to connect local to national and world history. First, as the walking tour indicates, students can physically visit a place. Reading about the presidential election of Barack Obama or the Vietnam War protests is one thing. Actually walking where these events took place is quite another experience. Students stand where history occurred, making it more real and more personal. Their senses are engaged. They see, hear, smell, touch, and possibly taste what it might have been like to be where history unfolded. The students, the teacher, family, or friends may even have participated in the event—or had relatives that did.

Second, because visiting is not always possible, virtual tours provide students with a reasonable facsimile. YouTube and other sites house videos of places including the Ziggurat of the Sumerian city of Ur in present-day Iraq and the Battle of Oriskany.[1]

In addition, as is the case with any inquiry, students study other print and visual resources. Whether examined in person, viewed in a video, or studied using photos, pictures, maps, or print reading, the physical places and structures are primary sources. Students build literacy skills by reading, analyzing, and interpreting places, buildings, statues, and perhaps the land or waterways. Basically, any assignment students typically do can be adapted to integrate the local perspective. The physical artifacts can be primary source examples for document-based questions (DBQ). Students can develop walking tours in person or virtually. They can write research papers or participate in simulations.

A key is recognizing possibilities, identifying local examples to integrate into history courses. In some cases, history is just outside the front door or a short car ride away to a historic building or site that played an important role in U.S. history. Boston's Freedom Trail is one example, as is Independence Hall in Philadelphia where the Declaration of Independence was signed. Battlegrounds are popular tourist destinations and excellent primary sources for study. Buildings, statues, parks, and waterways, virtually everything in a local area, might have historical significance.

In many cities across the nation, the diverse narratives of history are evident. Little Italy, Hester Street, Harlem, and other New York City neighborhoods are witnesses to the ongoing immigration and settlement of various racial and ethnic groups over time. Other cities have similar neighborhoods where racial and ethnic groups clustered in the past or do so today. The various "towns" with ethnic names are a good example. Often a local historical society or museum provides resources into the history of a specific racial or ethnic group.

There are also the statues, buildings, and other structures that have historical significance. For example, the Edmund Pettus Bridge in Selma, Alabama, played a major role in the civil rights movement and is a National Historical Landmark. Ironically, constructed in 1940, the bridge commemorates Edmund Pettus. Inquiring into who Pettis was, students learn he was a Confederate general, a leader of the Ku Klux Klan in Alabama, and a U.S. senator.

Bretton Woods

At times, history appears in what seem unlikely places. The Mount Washington Hotel (currently owned by Omni) is located in the Bretton Woods ski resort area of the White Mountains of New Hampshire. History teachers know Bretton Woods was an important place during World War II. In July 1944, delegates from 45 nations met at the hotel and agreed to create the International Monetary Fund and what became the World Bank. This attempt to plan for the postwar world was a rehearsal of sorts for the international cooperation that created the United Nations. Hotel guests and visitors can visit the room where the Bretton Wood agreement was signed.[2]

Classroom Activities

In a World War II unit, students can gain insight into how places with a very different purpose also served important historical needs and how those places memorialize their historical connection. One idea is to use the Mount Washington Hotel's ski resort function as a hook, asking students why they are looking at the resort while studying World War II. As students conduct research into the hotel, they will discover the Bretton Woods connection, so they can learn that history occurs in everyday places. They can also learn the ongoing significance of the Bretton Conference by briefly looking at the role the International Monetary Fund plays today.

The above discussion shows that in any local community, connections to history abound. Bringing the local perspective into the study of history enhances its relevance for students. In some cases, the local community is far removed from the student but has special significance because it connects to historical topics and themes over time. Memorials and tourist spots in particular have special appeal. Other times, everyday places offer similar opportunities for students to connect local people, places, and events to what they are studying. The following examples are the proverbial tip of the iceberg of potential local examples to use in history courses.

EXPLORING CHANGING CONNECTIONS OVER TIME

In some cases, the local focus of study served several important purposes over time. By examining changing roles and significance, students can return to the local focus in different units of study. In the process, they gain insight into the theme of change and continuity.

Arlington National Cemetery (Arlington)

Located just outside of Washington DC in Arlington, Virginia, Arlington National Cemetery has a long and storied history. Today, it is one of two national cemeteries maintained by the U.S. Army in the United States. Almost 400,000 people are buried in the 639-acre cemetery. But its history dates back much farther and connects to George Washington, Robert E. Lee, and several other important people, places, and events in U.S. history.

Initially, George Washington Custis, the adopted grandson of George Washington, developed the land to be an estate worked by enslaved people. Mary Custis Washington was his grandmother. Custis inherited the land from his natural father. He married Mary Lee and their daughter later married Robert E. Lee. Upon Custis's death in 1857, the estate passed to his daughter.

After the Civil War started, the U.S. Army occupied and later confiscated the estate. During the war, the estate supported thousands of African Americans who had fled enslavement. In 1863, the federal government established a Freedman's Village that eventually became a community of 1,500 people. It included two churches, schools, a home for the elderly, and a hospital. The Village was closed in 1900 when the land was added to Arlington National Cemetery, which had been established in 1864. The cemetery was segregated until 1948 when President Harry S. Truman integrated the armed forces.

As the Arlington National Cemetery website notes, military personnel from every major U.S. war are buried at the cemetery, concluding that "the history of our nation is reflected on the grounds of the cemetery."[3]

Classroom Activities

Arlington National Cemetery spans several historical topics including George Washington, enslavement, the experiences of ex-enslaved people, the Civil War, and almost every other major U.S. war. Using the geographic concept of place as a location with unique significance, teachers can connect to studies of various topics across a course to gauge how the special features that made Arlington a place changed over time to meet new needs.

Arlington offers several options for classroom activities. By constructing a timeline of Arlington from the early 1800s to the present, students answer an important historical question: How and why do changing times, attitudes, and needs affect the purpose and significance of a place? In answering this question, students could assume the personalities of people who lived at that time and write journals or biographies describing their lives at Arlington over time.

Another possibility is to explore the Freedmen's Village experience as a metaphor for race relations during the Civil War, the Reconstruction era, the era of segregation, and from 1948 to the present. Freedman's Village also provides an opportunity for students to inquire into how and why African Americans created communities after the Civil War. Here, too, journals or biographies of people who lived at Freedman's Village are possible assignments, as are publications and videos.

Logan Statue, Grant Park, Chicago, Illinois

The statue of General John Alexander Logan seated on a horse is located in Chicago's Grant Park just east of the corner of Michigan Avenue and 9th Street. Both the man memorialized and the statue connect to several topics in U.S. history. John Alexander Logan was born in Illinois in 1826. He served in the Mexican American War and then practiced law before entering politics as a Democratic Illinois State representative and then as a congressional representative. When the Civil War started, he joined the army as a colonel but was promoted to general, fighting in several battles including Vicksburg.

After the Civil War, Logan joined the Republican Party and was elected senator from Illinois. He also was Republican presidential candidate John G. Blaine's choice for vice president in 1884, though they lost the election. Logan was involved in veteran's affairs, serving as head of the Grand Army of the Republic. He played an important role in establishing the Memorial Day holiday in 1868. Logan died in 1886.

Logan's statue was installed in 1897. It was created by two prominent sculptors. Auguste Saint-Gaudens sculpted Logan while Alexander Phimister Proctor created his horse. During the 1968 Democratic Convention in

Chicago and afterward, the statue was a rallying place for anti-Vietnam War protesters.[4]

Classroom Activities

As was the case with Arlington National Cemetery, Logan Statue offers similar opportunities for inquiry-based classroom opportunities. Another activity is to ask students to research Logan and his life, connecting him to such topics as the Mexican American War, politics before and after the Civil War, and the creation of Memorial Day. They could construct a personal and topical timeline to answer the following question: Why or why not do you think John Alexander Logan deserves to have a statue in Grant Park? A different activity is to ask students to research Logan's life and have them infer what Logan's position might have been on the Vietnam War and the antiwar protests?

EXAMINING THE LOCAL COMMUNITY, EVERYDAY LIFE, AND RELEVANCE

So far, the discussion has shown that if you look for it, history is everywhere. A city street, a resort hotel, a national cemetery, and a statue in a park connect to important U.S. and world historical topics. What about aspects of a student's life? How can a teacher connect what students meet every day in a local community to what they study in a history classroom to increase the relevance of what students learn?

Too often, the commonplace, what is met in an everyday routine is overlooked as having a historical connection. Names of local communities, streets, buildings, schools, and parks, among other things, often offer teachers opportunities to make local connections. The same is true of aspects of the built environment such as roadways, buildings, bridges, and so on. This chapter opened noting the importance of the Edmund Pettus Bridge in Selma, Alabama. Aspects of the natural environment, such as waterways or landforms, are other examples. Similarly, a neighborhood and the people in it also connect to historical topics and themes.

The discussion here looks at names, the built and natural environment, and neighborhoods to explore ways to integrate the local community into history education. The classroom activities involve students inquiring into various topics using maps, photos, perhaps drawings, and other resources. They also might use buildings and other structures, and geographic features as primary sources, learning how to read and analyze them in the process. As a result, students become much more aware not just of their surroundings but also how to assess their value and significance.

What's in a Name?

Every day, teachers and students travel on streets and avenues with names or go to schools, many of which also have names. Many of these names are familiar. Students know who many of the the people are and why they are historically significant. Other names are less familiar though not necessarily lacking significance. The closeness to student lives makes these roadway and school names prime examples for connecting the local community to U.S. or world history.

Often streets are named after presidents or other famous public figures. How many communities have a street, avenue, or boulevard named Washington, Madison, Franklin, Lincoln, or King? In some case, streets, or a segment of them, are named after prominent people. Some examples include Miles Davis Way and Humphrey Bogart Avenue in New York City, and Edgar Martinez Drive in Seattle and Ida B. Wells Drive in Chicago. (Very few women have streets named after them.)

Similarly, many schools are named after famous people. Sometimes, the school name fits the neighborhood and the purpose of the school. Emma Lazarus High School in New York City is named after the woman who wrote the poem inscribed on the Statue of Liberty. The school is on Hester Street, once a destination for Jewish immigrants. Lazarus High School is fittingly for English language scholars.[5] The connections to immigration span over a century.

Students attending Cesar Chavez High School in Phoenix, Arizona, can connect their studies of labor unions and social activism to the Mexican American labor leader. Seventy percent of the students attending the high school are Hispanic.

In some cases, the school is named after a less well-known individual. On Chicago's north side, students attend Stephen Tyng Mather High School. Mather was an early 20th-century industrialist and conservationist. He played a strong role in the creation of the National Park Service and became its first director.[6] When studying the conservation movement of the early 1900s or the environmental movement of today, the topic gains greater relevance when Mather students study their school's namesake.

Classroom Activities

Names mean something. Connecting names of streets and schools to historical studies makes them more relevant for students living in that local community or attending that school. The streets and schools can be used to spark inquiry into a topic. Students can research the people whose names grace the street or school as part of their inquiry. A possible question to explore is why was this street or school named after this person?

The Built and Natural Environment

Whether it be a building, a roadway, a river, a lake, or other geographic feature, the built and natural environment also provides promising local connections to teaching and learning history. Here, too, names can be of value, but the structure or natural feature may also have historical significance in relation to an event, movement, trend, and so on.

Buildings

In some cases, a house, building, or bridge such as Edmund Pettus are sites where historical figures lived or important events occurred. In Boston, numerous historical places exist. Students at Liberty High School are a half mile from the Paul Revere House. They are just over a half mile from the Old North Church where Revere was sent the message regarding British troop movements that led to his famous ride and the Battle of Lexington. While studying the American Revolution, field trips to Revere's house and the church show students that history happened in their neighborhood bringing them closer to the events they study.

Railroads and Highways

Buildings are not the only parts of the built environment that act as primary sources to provide a local perspective to history. Rails and roads have played a huge role in the development of local communities, the United States, and other nations. In addition to moving people and goods, including immigrants coming to new communities, rails and roadways spurred development of many urban, suburban, and rural communities.

Proximity to a railroad or highway influence the well-being of a community. Chicago's development into a major city was fueled by its status as a railroad center. The freeway system in Southern California played a substantial role in the growth of Los Angeles and surrounding communities. Millions of people ride commuter trains or drive on highways for work, shopping, entertainment, and other reasons. How many of you use railroads or highways regularly?

Railroads, including railroad stations, and highways provide excellent opportunities for students to study history using local connections. Immigration is one example. After arriving in the United States, railroads carried immigrants to communities throughout the nation. African American and white migrants from rural areas often rode trains to the cities where they settled. Especially after World War II, highways performed a similar function. By exploring the railroads and highways serving their communities, students learn how new settlers, perhaps their own families, came to their communities to live.

The rise of suburbia is another example. After World War II, the construction of highways fueled the growth of older communities and the creation of new suburbs. Using the transportation systems serving their communities as an example, students gain a local perspective on the influence of transportation on post–World War II development.

Classroom Activities

Beyond the usual DBQs and presentations, buildings, railroads, and roadways offer students opportunities to apply geography themes in their study of history. Why is a building located where it is? How does a building's architecture and purpose help characterize its location as a historic place? The historical themes of change and continuity also can be examined. How and why did a building's purpose change or remain the same over time? Such questions ask students to inquire into local history and connect their findings to larger historical topics, themes, and trends.

Similar questions stimulate inquiry into railroads and roadways, but the pivotal role transportation plays opens other options. Applying geography themes, students can assess how and why these systems affected their community's development. How did the development of transportations systems influence the community's development as a place? How does the theme of movement help us understand how and why transportation affects a community? Using the theme of human-environmental interaction, students learn how and why the construction of the rail and road system, especially highways, impact areas in their path.

The triad of inquiry, primary sources, and literacy guides students as they answer these questions. Students consult maps, plans, and other visual and print sources to answer these questions. As their study progressing, they practice important literacy skills.

Neighborhoods

Whether it be in a city, town, suburb, or rural area, students live in a neighborhood that forms their local community. Cities, suburbs, towns, villages, and rural areas are also local communities, but neighborhoods have a special cachet since they often comprise much if not all of a student's experience. Students live, play, go to school, and possibly work in a neighborhood. All neighborhoods have historical value if students learn how to connect where they live to large historical topics and themes.

For example, in U.S. history, the Harlem Renaissance is a major topic. The stress typically is on the cultural renaissance. But, as an African American community, Harlem's importance extends beyond the renaissance era of the 1920s and 1930s. Its history has reflected much of the nation's history.

In some cases, neighborhoods have been destinations for different immigrants over time. In Chicago, Pilsen has been a microcosm of sorts for the different waves of immigration from the mid-1800s to the 21st century. In the 1840s, the Pilsen neighborhood on the south side was initially home to German and Irish immigrants. After the Civil War, Bohemian, Polish, and other Eastern European immigrants moved to the neighborhood that then became known as Pilsen, after the Czech city. In the 1960s, Mexican families moved to the area, becoming the dominant ethnic group.

Classroom Activities

Neighborhoods offer excellent inquiry opportunities for students. Using the major content areas of social studies (political, economic, and social systems, geography, and history), students can construct neighborhood profiles that include connections to larger historical movements and themes. In the process, they gain greater insight into how the development of the neighborhood fits in the larger scheme of things.

Regarding Harlem and Pilsen, two ideas seem viable. First, while studying the Harlem Renaissance, ask students to profile the neighborhood's history, political, economic, and sociocultural development through the 1930s. In this way, students gain greater insight into the community context that gave rose to the movement. Second, students can extend their study to profile Harlem today and compare the findings for the Renaissance era to assess what has changed and what has remained the same. The study of Pilsen can involve similar activities but focus more on immigration and cultural changes over time.

CONCLUSION

Numerous ways exist to integrate the local community into history teaching and learning. Doing so brings history home to students, increasing the relevance of their studies. What happened and who lived there is not remote, rather it happened where they live.

NOTES

1. Buck Rogers 2000, "Ziggurat of Ur Tour" (May–September 2007), YouTube, https://www.youtube.com/watch?v=MB7i1h3whn4; Exploring with Dan, "Battle of Oriskany!," YouTube (August 21, 2021), https://www.youtube.com/watch?v=UfkmPr_2fZU.

2. A newsreel of the Bretton Woods Conference showing the Mount Washington Hotel is available on YouTube. Daniel, J. B. Mitchell, "1944 Bretton Woods International Monetary Conference," https://youtube.com/watch?v=GVytOtfPZe8.

3. "History of Arlington National Cemetery," Arlington National Cemetery, https://www.arlingtoncemetery.mil/Explore/History-of-Arlington-National-Cemetery.

4. "John Alexander Logan Monument," Chicago Park District, https://www.chicagoparkdistrict.com/parks-facilities/john-alexander-logan-monument.

5. Emma Lazarus School for English Language Scholars, https://www.emmalazarus.org/home_page.

6. "Stephen Tyng Mather," National Park Service, https://www.nps.gov/people/stephen-tyng-mather.htm.

Conclusion

Teaching history involves learning history, not just gaining content knowledge or understanding current educational ideas and trends. Teaching history involves bringing subject matter and pedagogical knowledge together to create relevant, meaningful, and effective learning. In today's environment, teaching history also involves accommodating the politics of the history culture wars.

The triad of inquiry, primary sources, and literacy offers teachers a method to navigate the various challenges teaching history faces by meeting the goal of preparing active, competent citizens. Inquiry engages students in critical thinking to make informed conclusions supported by evidence. Primary sources are the mother lode of information students study to answer important questions. Literacy comprises the skills students need to conduct inquiry and analyze primary sources.

Inquiry also helps teachers organize massive amounts of historical content into manageable "chunks" for learning. Questions focus student learning on relevant topics while content themes provide examples for the inquiry. The questions also pique student interests, motivating learning.

Primary sources are the slippery resources that students use to inquire. They bring students closer to the people, places, and events being studied but do so with a caution. The subjective, incomplete nature of primary sources means students must interrogate them to ensure they are what they claim to be. Students also need to verify the story primary sources tell. Each primary source is one piece of a larger inquiry puzzle that students complete.

Literacy makes it all happen. Inquiry and primary source study engage students in reading, analyzing, interpreting, evaluating, organizing, making sense of, and communicating. The inquiry process climbs Bloom's revised taxonomy. Over time, the ongoing practice of inquiry and studying primary sources improves student skills proficiency.

Because students control their learning, coming to their own conclusions based on broad-based evidence, in most cases, the triad can elevate history teachers above the culture wars fray. Good history teaching and learning does not begin, proceed, or end with a predetermined political agenda or conclusion. Yes, history can be messy and inhumane, but its study also shows how people responded to the mess and inhumanity to try and improve their lives. The teacher's job is to set the context and process for learning to proceed. The student's task is to make sense of what they learned and come to an evidence-backed conclusion.

Hopefully, this book has provided some ideas, methods, and examples to ensure every student gets a first-class history education.

About the Author

Mark Newman is professor of social studies education at National College of Education, National Louis University in Chicago. He primarily teaches social studies methods and secondary education courses. Newman has published articles and books on social studies, history, geography, primary sources, and visual literacy. He has been director of several National Endowment for the Humanities grants and directed a Library of Congress Teaching with Primary Sources grant. In 2016, he won the National College of Education Distinguished Teaching Award and, in 2022, he won the International Visual Literacy Association Award.

Mark Newman is editor of the Rowman & Littlefield series Teaching History Today and in the Future. This book is the first volume in the series.

www.ingramcontent.com/pod-product-compliance
Lightning Source LLC
Chambersburg PA
CBHW021851300426
44115CB00005B/112